Welcome to JUMP Math!

T0275049

Entering the world of JUMP Math means believing that every learner to be fully numerate and love math.

The **JUMP Math Accumula Student Book** is the companion to the **JUMP Math Accumula** supplementary resource for Grades 1 to 8, which is designed to strengthen foundational math knowledge and prepare all students for success in understanding math problems at grade level. This book provides opportunities for students to consolidate learning by exploring important math concepts through independent practice.

Unique Evidence-Based Approach and Resources

JUMP Math's unique approach, Kindergarten to Grade 8 resources, and professional learning for teachers have been producing positive learning outcomes for children and teachers in classrooms in Canada, the United States, and other countries for over 20 years. Our resources are aligned with the science on how children's brains learn best and have been demonstrated through studies to greatly improve problem solving, computation, and fluency skills. (See our research at **jumpmath.org**.) Our approach is designed to build equity by supporting the full spectrum of learners to achieve success in math.

Confidence Building is Key

JUMP Math begins each grade with review to enable every student to quickly develop the confidence needed to engage deeply with math. Our distinctive incremental approach to learning math concepts gradually increases the level of difficulty for students, empowering them to become motivated, independent problem solvers. Our books are also designed with simple pictures and models to avoid overwhelming learners when introducing new concepts, enabling them to see the deep structure of the math and gain the confidence to solve a wide range of math problems.

About JUMP Math

JUMP Math is a non-profit organization dedicated to helping every child in every classroom develop confidence, understanding, and a love of math. JUMP Math also offers a comprehensive set of classroom resources for students in Kindergarten to Grade 8.

For more information, visit JUMP Math at: www.jumpmath.org.

Contents

Accumula 3

STUDENT BOOK

Copyright © 2014–2024 JUMP Math

Excerpts from this publication may be reproduced under licence from Access Copyright, or with the express written permission of JUMP Math, or as permitted by law.

All rights are otherwise reserved, and no part of this publication may be reproduced, stored in a retrieval system, or transmitted in any form or by any means, electronic, mechanical, photocopying, scanning, recording or otherwise, except as specifically authorized.

JUMP Math
One Yonge Street, Suite 1014
Toronto, Ontario M5E 1E5
Canada
www.jumpmath.org

Writers: Dr. Francisco Kibedi, Dr. John Mighton, Gregory Belostotski
Consultants: Dr. Anna Klebanov, Julie Lorinc, Dr. Sohrab Rahbar
Editors: Megan Burns, Liane Tsui, Natalie Francis, Annie Chern, Julia Cochrane, Janice Dyer, Neomi Majmudar, Una Malcolm, Jessica Pegis, Rita Vanden Heuvel
Layout and Illustrations: Linh Lam, Gabriella Kerr, Marijke Friesen, Ilyana Martinez, Vanessa Parson-Robbs
Cover Design: Sunday Lek
Cover Photograph: © vanakr/Freepik.com

ISBN 978-1-77395-295-6

First printing January 2024

Parts of this material were first published in 2014 in AP Book 3.1, US edition (978-1-927457-42-9) and AP Book 3.2, US edition (978-1-927457-43-6).

Printed and bound in Canada

1. Place Value—Ones, Tens, and Hundreds

You can write a number in a place value chart. Example: 431

Hundreds	Tens	Ones
4	3	1

1. Write the number in the place value chart.

	Hundreds	Tens	Ones
a) 65	0	6	5
c) 408			
e) 17			
g) 372			
i) 0			

	Hundreds	Tens	Ones
b) 283			
d) 130			
f) 4			
h) 900			
j) 825			

```
        3    7    5
        ↗    ↑    ↖
   hundreds  tens  ones
```

2. Write the place value of the underlined digit.

a) 1<u>7</u> [ones]   b) 9<u>8</u> [ ]   c) <u>2</u>4 [ ]

d) <u>6</u>3 [ ]   e) <u>3</u>81 [ ]   f) 97<u>2</u> [ ]

g) 4<u>2</u>5 [ ]   h) 25<u>6</u> [ ]   i) <u>1</u>08 [ ]

3. Write the place value of the digit 5.

a) 50 [tens]   b) 15 [ ]   c) 251 [ ]

d) 586 [ ]   e) 375 [ ]   f) 584 [ ]

g) 935 [ ]   h) 563 [ ]   i) 153 [ ]

COPYRIGHT © JUMP MATH: NOT TO BE COPIED. US EDITION

The number 586 is a **3-digit number**.

- The **digit** 5 stands for 500.
- The **digit** 8 stands for 80.
- The **digit** 6 stands for 6.

4. Fill in the blank.

a) In the number 657, the **digit** 5 stands for ___50___.

b) In the number 248, the **digit** 2 stands for _____.

c) In the number 129, the **digit** 9 stands for _____.

d) In the number 108, the **digit** 0 stands for _____.

e) In the number 803, the digit _____ is in the **hundreds** place.

f) In the number 596, the digit _____ is in the **tens** place.

g) In the number 410, the digit _____ is in the **ones** place.

5. What number does each digit stand for?

a)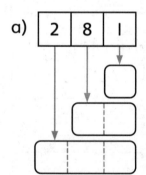

b)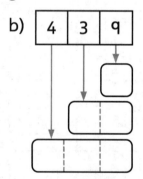

c)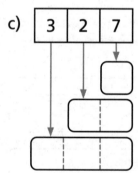

6. What number does the digit 3 stand for?

a) 237 [30]   b) 638 [   ]   c) 326 [   ]

d) 403 [   ]   e) 309 [   ]   f) 883 [   ]

g) 379 [   ]   h) 31 [   ]   i) 543 [   ]

j) 135 [   ]   k) 3 [   ]   l) 374 [   ]

COPYRIGHT © JUMP MATH: NOT TO BE COPIED. US EDITION

JUMP Math Accumula

2. Base Ten Blocks

	Hundreds block	Tens block	Ones block
	= 100	= 10	□ = 1

1. Write the number of hundreds, tens, and ones. Then write the number.

	Hundreds	Tens	Ones	Number
a)	1	3	6	136
b)				
c)				
d)				
e)				

COPYRIGHT © JUMP MATH: NOT TO BE COPIED. US EDITION

2. Sketch the number using base ten blocks.

a) 342

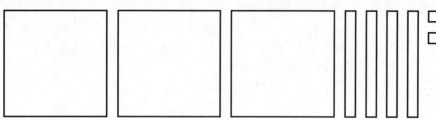

b) 237

c) 113

d) 206

e) 130

COPYRIGHT © JUMP MATH: NOT TO BE COPIED. US EDITION

3. Sketch the missing base ten blocks.

a) 583

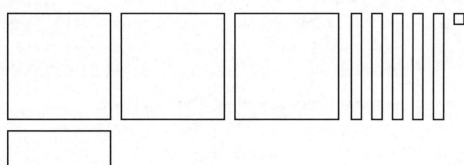

b) 467

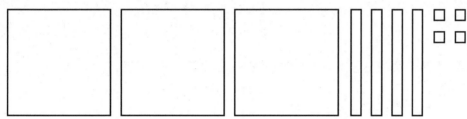

4. Fill in the blanks.

a) 472 has ___4___ hundreds, ___7___ tens, and ___2___ ones.

b) 573 has _____ hundreds, _____ tens, and _____ ones.

c) 821 has _____ hundreds, _____ tens, and _____ one.

d) 409 has _____ hundreds, _____ tens, and _____ ones.

BONUS ▶ 3 has _____ hundreds, _____ tens, and _____ ones.

5. How many more tens blocks do you need to draw 452 than to draw 422? Explain.

COPYRIGHT © JUMP MATH: NOT TO BE COPIED. US EDITION

3. Expanded Form

You can write the number **475** in **expanded form** in two ways.
- Using numerals and words: **4 hundreds** + **7 tens** + **5 ones**
- Using numerals only: **400** + **70** + **5**

1. Write "hundreds," "tens," or "ones" for each digit. Then write in expanded form.

   a) 658   6 _hundreds_   b) 493   4 _____

           5 _tens_   9 _____

           8 _ones_   3 _____

     _600_ + _50_ + _8_   _____ + _____ + _____

2. Fill in the blanks.

   a) 267 = _2_ hundreds + _6_ tens + _7_ ones

   b) 381 = _____ hundreds + _____ tens + _____ one

   c) 709 = _____ hundreds + _____ ones

   d) 727 = _____ hundreds + _____ tens + _____ ones

   e) 53 = _____ tens + _____ ones

   f) 640 = _____ hundreds + _____ tens

3. Write the number in expanded form using numerals and words.

   a) 547 = _5 hundreds + 4 tens + 7 ones_____

   b) 239 = _____

   c) 73 = _____

   d) 190 = _____

   e) 605 = _____

   f) 420 = _____

COPYRIGHT © JUMP MATH: NOT TO BE COPIED. US EDITION

4. Write the number for the expanded form.

   a) 3 hundreds + 4 tens + 7 ones

   | 347 |

   b) 9 hundreds + 8 tens + 2 ones

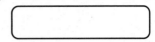

   c) 5 tens + 6 ones

   d) 2 hundreds + 7 tens

   e) 6 hundreds + I ten + 4 ones

   f) I hundred + 8 ones

5. Write the number in expanded form using numerals only.

   a) 762 = ___700 + 60 + 2_____

   b) 845 = _____

   c) 72 = _____

   d) 503 = _____

   e) 431 = _____

   f) 978 = _____

6. Write the number for the expanded form.

   a) 400 + 50 + 3 = ___453___

   b) 800 + 70 + I = _____

   c) 40 + 8 = _____

   d) 600 + 20 = _____

   e) 900 + I = _____

   f) 400 + 40 + 4 = _____

   g) 500 + 40 + 9 = _____

   h) 300 + I0 + 5 = _____

7. Write the missing numbers for the expanded form.

   a) 247 = 200 + ___40___ + 7

   b) 598 = 500 + 90 + _____

   c) 651 = _____ + 50 + I

   d) 843 = 800 + _____ + _____

   e) 352 = _____ + 50 + _____

   f) 400 + 50 + _____ = 458

   g) 300 + _____ + 7 = 367

   h) _____ + 2 = 702

   i) 57 = _____ + 7

   j) 700 + 80 + _____ = 788

   k) _____ + 20 + _____ = 924

   l) _____ + _____ + _____ = 835

COPYRIGHT © JUMP MATH: NOT TO BE COPIED. US EDITION

4. Regrouping of Ones, Tens, and Hundreds

You can **regroup** 10 ones blocks as 1 tens block.

10 ones = 1 ten   12 ones = 1 ten + 2 ones

1. Circle each group of 10 ones blocks. How many ones are left?

   a)   b)   c)   d)

   __5__ ones left   _____ ones left   _____ ones left   _____ ones left

2. Regroup each group of 10 ones as 1 tens block. Draw the new number.

	Before	After
a)		
c)		

	Before	After
b)		
d)		

3. Regroup 10 ones blocks as 1 tens block. Draw the new number.
   Then fill in the blanks.

	Blocks	Numbers and Words
a) Before		__4__ tens + __13__ ones
After		_____ tens + _____ ones
b) Before		_____ tens + _____ ones
After		_____ tens + _____ ones

COPYRIGHT © JUMP MATH: NOT TO BE COPIED. US EDITION

You can regroup 10 tens blocks as 1 hundreds block.

10 tens = 1 hundred   12 tens = 1 hundred + 2 tens

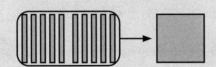   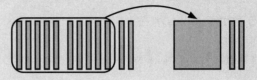

4. Circle each group of 10 tens blocks. How many tens are left?

a) 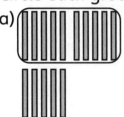   b)    c)    d)

_5_ tens left   _____ tens left   _____ tens left   _____ tens left

5. Regroup 10 tens blocks as 1 hundreds block. Draw the new number.
   Then fill in the blanks.

	Blocks	Numbers and Words
a) Before		_1_ hundred + _13_ tens + _3_ ones
After		____ hundreds + _____ tens + ____ ones
b) Before		____ hundred + _____ tens + ____ ones
After		____ hundreds + _____ tens + ____ ones
c) Before		____ hundred + _____ tens + ____ ones
After		_____ hundreds + _____ tens + ____ ones

COPYRIGHT © JUMP MATH: NOT TO BE COPIED. US EDITION

6. Write the total number of tens or ones.

   a) 4 hundreds + 2 tens = __42__ tens   b) 2 hundreds + 7 tens = _____ tens

   c) 5 tens + 7 ones = _____ ones   d) 3 hundreds + 0 tens = _____ tens

   e) I hundred + I ten = _____ tens   f) 6 tens + 0 ones = _____ ones

7. Regroup. Then fill in the blanks.

   a) 3 tens + 12 ones = 4 tens + __2__ ones

   b) 5 hundreds + 14 tens = 6 hundreds + _____ tens

   c) 5 tens + 14 ones = _____ tens + 4 ones

   d) 3 hundreds + 11 tens = 4 hundreds + _____ ten

   e) 4 tens + _____ ones = 5 tens + 3 ones

   f) _____ hundred + 18 tens = 2 hundreds + 8 tens

   g) _____ tens + 17 ones = 4 tens + 7 ones

   h) 7 hundreds + 19 tens = _____ hundreds + 9 ones

8. Regroup. Then fill in the blanks.

   a) 3 hundreds + 5 tens + 14 ones = 3 hundreds + _____ tens + 4 ones

   b) 4 hundreds + 16 tens + 7 ones = _____ hundreds + 6 tens + 7 ones

   c) I hundred + 13 tens + 4 ones = _____ hundreds + 3 tens + 4 ones

   d) 5 hundreds + 2 tens + 19 ones = 5 hundreds + _____ tens + 9 ones

   e) 2 hundreds + 3 tens + 15 ones = _____ hundreds + 4 tens + 5 ones

   f) 7 hundreds + 8 tens + 13 ones = 7 hundreds + 9 tens + _____ ones

9. Draw base ten models to show the regrouping of ones, tens, and hundreds in Question 8.a).

COPYRIGHT © JUMP MATH: NOT TO BE COPIED. US EDITION

5. Addition with Regrouping—Tens

1. Find the **sum** by drawing the blocks and by adding the digits.

a) 24 + 15

	With Blocks		With Digits	
	Tens	**Ones**	**Tens**	**Ones**
24	‖	⠿	2	4
15	|	⠿	1	5
Sum	‖|	⠿	3	9

24 + 15 = _____

b) 62 + 21

	With Blocks		With Digits	
	Tens	**Ones**	**Tens**	**Ones**
62	‖‖‖	⠿		
21	‖	⠿		
Sum				

62 + 21 = _____

c) 29 + 50

	With Blocks		With Digits	
	Tens	**Ones**	**Tens**	**Ones**
29	‖	⠿		
50	‖‖‖			
Sum				

29 + 50 = _____

d) 36 + 23

	With Blocks		With Digits	
	Tens	**Ones**	**Tens**	**Ones**
36	‖|	⠿		
23	‖	⠿		
Sum				

36 + 23 = _____

2. Add the numbers by adding the digits. Start in the ones place.

a)
```
  2 3
+ 1 2
-----
```
b)
```
  4 8
+ 2 1
-----
```
c)
```
  6 3
+ 3 6
-----
```
d)
```
  4 3
+ 4 5
-----
```
e)
```
  8 7
+ 1 0
-----
```

COPYRIGHT © JUMP MATH: NOT TO BE COPIED. US EDITION

3. Find the **sum** by drawing the blocks and by adding the digits.
Then regroup.

a) 14 + 38

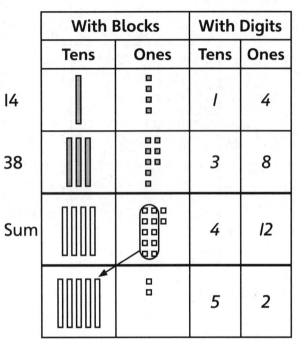

	With Blocks		With Digits	
	Tens	**Ones**	**Tens**	**Ones**
14			1	4
38			3	8
Sum			4	12
			5	2

14 + 38 = _____

b) 19 + 12

	With Blocks		With Digits	
	Tens	**Ones**	**Tens**	**Ones**
19				
12				
Sum				

19 + 12 = _____

c) 27 + 34

	With Blocks		With Digits	
	Tens	**Ones**	**Tens**	**Ones**
27				
34				
Sum				

27 + 34 = _____

d) 48 + 7

	With Blocks		With Digits	
	Tens	**Ones**	**Tens**	**Ones**
48				
7				
Sum				

48 + 7 = _____

COPYRIGHT © JUMP MATH: NOT TO BE COPIED. US EDITION

4. Add the ones digits. Then fill in the blanks.

a)
```
  [1]  ▨
   5  8
 +  1  4
 ▨ | 2 |
```

b)
```
  [ ]  ▨
   3  6
 +  4  7
 ▨ |   |
```

c)
```
  [ ]  ▨
   1  5
 +  2  8
 ▨ |   |
```

d)
```
  [ ]  ▨
   3  5
 +  4  8
 ▨ |   |
```

e)
```
  [ ]  ▨
   2  7
 +     5
 ▨ |   |
```

f)
```
  [ ]  ▨
   4  8
 +  2  8
 ▨ |   |
```

g)
```
  [ ]  ▨
   2  5
 +  3  5
 ▨ |   |
```

h)
```
  [ ]  ▨
   2  7
 +  4  9
 ▨ |   |
```

5. Add the numbers in the tens place.

a)
```
  [1]  ▨
   5  8
 +  1  4
 | 7 | 2 |
```

b)
```
  [1]  ▨
   1  6
 +  2  7
 |   | 3 |
```

c)
```
  [1]  ▨
   1  4
 +  1  6
 |   | 0 |
```

d)
```
  [1]  ▨
   2  5
 +  2  9
 |   | 4 |
```

e)
```
  [1]  ▨
   1  7
 +     8
 |   | 5 |
```

f)
```
  [1]  ▨
   3  7
 +  5  7
 |   | 4 |
```

g)
```
  [1]  ▨
   4  5
 +  4  5
 |   | 0 |
```

h)
```
  [1]  ▨
   2  3
 +  6  9
 |   | 2 |
```

6. Add the numbers by regrouping.

a)
```
  [1]  ▨
   3  7
 +  3  6
 | 7 | 3 |
```

b)
```
  [ ]  ▨
   1  6
 +  4  5
 |   |   |
```

c)
```
  [ ]  ▨
   3  2
 +  1  9
 |   |   |
```

d)
```
  [ ]  ▨
   2  7
 +  5  8
 |   |   |
```

7. Use grid paper to line up the digits. (Put ones under ones, tens under tens.) Then add by regrouping.

a) 29 + 5   b) 46 + 26   c) 31 + 49   d) 55 + 28

COPYRIGHT © JUMP MATH: NOT TO BE COPIED. US EDITION

6. Addition with Regrouping—Hundreds

I. Add by adding the ones, tens, and hundreds.

a)
```
    2  3  4
  + 3  5  2
```
                 ___ hundreds + ___ tens + ___ ones

\+ ___ hundreds + ___ tens + ___ ones

= ___ hundreds + ___ tens + ___ ones

b)
```
    4  7  2
  + 5  1  6
```
                 ___ hundreds + ___ tens + ___ ones

\+ ___ hundreds + ___ ten + ___ ones

= ___ hundreds + ___ tens + ___ ones

c)
```
    1  0  8
  + 5  2  1
```
                 ___ hundred + ___ tens + ___ ones

\+ ___ hundreds + ___ tens + ___ one

= ___ hundreds + ___ tens + ___ ones

2. Add the digits. Start in the ones place.

a)
```
    2  9  5
  + 3  0  2
```
b)
```
    4  2  3
  + 2  6  1
```
c)
```
    3  1  2
  +    5  7
```
d)
```
    5  5  5
  + 4  4  4
```

e)
```
    3  4  7
  + 5  0  2
```
f)
```
    1  2  5
  + 3  6  4
```
g)
```
    4  2  3
  + 2  3  5
```
h)
```
    6  3  1
  + 2  2  7
```

i)
```
    4  2  8
  +    6  1
```
j)
```
    2  3  5
  + 5  0  0
```
k)
```
    4  2  3
  + 3  3  6
```
l)
```
    1  1  5
  + 2  6  1
```

m)
```
    1  3  1
  + 1  3  1
```
n)
```
    3  2  8
  +    6  1
```
o)
```
    9  8  9
  +    1  0
```
p)
```
    4  7  3
  + 4  2  4
```

COPYRIGHT © JUMP MATH: NOT TO BE COPIED. US EDITION

3. Add. You will need to regroup tens as hundreds.

a)
```
    2   3   4
  + 3   8   2
  _____
```

____ hundreds   +   ____ tens   +   ____ ones

+   ____ hundreds   +   ____ tens   +   ____ ones
_____

=   ____ hundreds   +   ____ tens   +   ____ ones

after regrouping   =   ____ hundreds   +   ____ ten   +   ____ ones

b)
```
    5   8   7
  + 2   5   2
  _____
```

____ hundreds   +   ____ tens   +   ____ ones

+   ____ hundreds   +   ____ tens   +   ____ ones
_____

=   ____ hundreds   +   ____ tens   +   ____ ones

after regrouping   =   ____ hundreds   +   ____ tens   +   ____ ones

4. Add. You will need to regroup tens as hundreds.

a)
```
  [ / ]
    3   7   5
  + 1   8   1
  _____
    5   5   6
```

b)
```
  [   ]
    1   9   6
  + 2   4   1
  _____
```

c)
```
  [   ]
    1   8   4
  + 1   8   5
  _____
```

d)
```
  [   ]
    2   4   5
  + 2   8   3
  _____
```

5. Add. You will need to regroup ones as tens.

a)
```
      [   ]
    1   4   7
  + 5   3   8
  _____
```

b)
```
      [   ]
    3   6   7
  + 5   1   7
  _____
```

c)
```
      [   ]
    4   3   5
  + 4   3   5
  _____
```

d)
```
      [   ]
    2   2   3
  + 6   4   9
  _____
```

6. Write the numbers in the grid. Then find the sum by regrouping.

a) 725 + 168   b) 250 + 450   c) 649 + 216   d) 491 + 323

	7	2	5																
+	1	6	8																

COPYRIGHT © JUMP MATH: NOT TO BE COPIED. US EDITION

7. Add. You will need to regroup twice.

a) 745 + 187

	/	/	
	7	4	5
+	1	8	7
	9	3	2

b) 368 + 498

	3	6	8
+	4	9	8

c) 649 + 276

	6	4	9
+	2	7	6

d) 587 + 123

	5	8	7
+	1	2	3

Sometimes the sum of two 2-digit numbers is a 3-digit number.

Example: 52 + 73

	5 tens	+	2 ones			5	2
+	7 tens	+	3 ones	or	+	7	3
	12 tens	+	5 ones			1	2	5

after regrouping = 1 hundred + **2** tens + **5** ones

---

8. Add the numbers. The answer will be a 3-digit number.

a)

	6	4
+	8	2

b)

	3	6
+	9	3

c)

	6	4
+	6	4

d)

	5	4
+	8	2

9. Add. You might need to regroup once or twice.

a)

	3	5	1
+	3	9	2

b)

	2	6	3
+		9	8

c)

	6	4	9
+	2	1	0

d)

	6	8	9
+	1	5	3

10. Add. Regroup where necessary.

a) 495 + 311   b) 526 + 269   c) 312 + 453   d) 555 + 294

11. Blanca has 164 toy cars. Ed has 87.
How many toy cars do they have in total?

COPYRIGHT © JUMP MATH: NOT TO BE COPIED. US EDITION

7. Subtraction without Regrouping

1. Subtract by crossing out tens and ones.

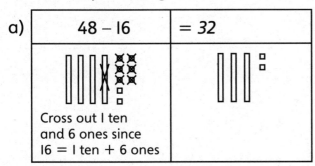

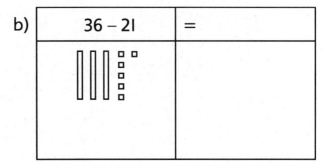

a) | 48 – 16 | = 32

Cross out 1 ten
and 6 ones since
16 = 1 ten + 6 ones

b) | 36 – 21 | =

c) | 25 – 13 | =

d) | 47 – 24 | =

2. Write the number of tens and ones in each number. Then subtract.

a) $\begin{array}{r} 49 = \underline{\ 4\ } \text{ tens} + \underline{\ 9\ } \text{ ones} \\ -\ 26 = \underline{\ 2\ } \text{ tens} + \underline{\ 6\ } \text{ ones} \\ \hline = \underline{\ 2\ } \text{ tens} + \underline{\ 3\ } \text{ ones} \\ = \underline{\ 23\ } \end{array}$

b) $\begin{array}{r} 59 = \underline{\ \ \ } \text{ tens} + \underline{\ \ \ } \text{ ones} \\ -\ 23 = \underline{\ \ \ } \text{ tens} + \underline{\ \ \ } \text{ ones} \\ \hline = \underline{\ \ \ } \text{ tens} + \underline{\ \ \ } \text{ ones} \\ = \underline{\ \ \ } \end{array}$

c) $\begin{array}{r} 67 = \underline{\ \ \ } \text{ tens} + \underline{\ \ \ } \text{ ones} \\ -\ 53 = \underline{\ \ \ } \text{ tens} + \underline{\ \ \ } \text{ ones} \\ \hline = \underline{\ \ \ } \text{ ten} + \underline{\ \ \ } \text{ ones} \\ = \underline{\ \ \ } \end{array}$

d) $\begin{array}{r} 86 = \underline{\ \ \ } \text{ tens} + \underline{\ \ \ } \text{ ones} \\ -\ 54 = \underline{\ \ \ } \text{ tens} + \underline{\ \ \ } \text{ ones} \\ \hline = \underline{\ \ \ } \text{ tens} + \underline{\ \ \ } \text{ ones} \\ = \underline{\ \ \ } \end{array}$

e) $\begin{array}{r} 97 = \underline{\ \ \ } \text{ tens} + \underline{\ \ \ } \text{ ones} \\ -\ 56 = \underline{\ \ \ } \text{ tens} + \underline{\ \ \ } \text{ ones} \\ \hline = \underline{\ \ \ } \text{ tens} + \underline{\ \ \ } \text{ one} \\ = \underline{\ \ \ } \end{array}$

f) $\begin{array}{r} 81 = \underline{\ \ \ } \text{ tens} + \underline{\ \ \ } \text{ one} \\ -\ 61 = \underline{\ \ \ } \text{ tens} + \underline{\ \ \ } \text{ one} \\ \hline = \underline{\ \ \ } \text{ tens} + \underline{\ \ \ } \text{ ones} \\ = \underline{\ \ \ } \end{array}$

COPYRIGHT © JUMP MATH: NOT TO BE COPIED. US EDITION

3. Write in expanded form using numerals only. Then subtract.

a)
$$
\begin{array}{rrrrr}
46 & = & 40 & + & 6 \\
- \ 32 & = & 30 & + & 2 \\
\hline
& = & 10 & + & 4 \\
& = & 14 &
\end{array}
$$

b)
$$
\begin{array}{rrl}
95 & = & \\
- \ 62 & = & \\
\hline
& = & \\
& = & \\
\end{array}
$$

c)
$$
\begin{array}{rrl}
37 & = & \\
- \ 11 & = & \\
\hline
& = & \\
& = & \\
\end{array}
$$

d)
$$
\begin{array}{rrl}
63 & = & \\
- \ 20 & = & \\
\hline
& = & \\
& = & \\
\end{array}
$$

e)
$$
\begin{array}{rrl}
29 & = & \\
- \ 14 & = & \\
\hline
& = & \\
& = & \\
\end{array}
$$

f)
$$
\begin{array}{rrl}
58 & = & \\
- \ 41 & = & \\
\hline
& = & \\
& = & \\
\end{array}
$$

4. Subtract the ones digits, then the tens digits.

a)
$$
\begin{array}{rr}
2 & 8 \\
- \ 1 & 2 \\
\hline
\end{array}
$$

b)
$$
\begin{array}{rr}
4 & 8 \\
- \ 2 & 7 \\
\hline
\end{array}
$$

c)
$$
\begin{array}{rr}
6 & 9 \\
- \ 5 & 3 \\
\hline
\end{array}
$$

d)
$$
\begin{array}{rr}
4 & 9 \\
- \ 4 & 5 \\
\hline
\end{array}
$$

e)
$$
\begin{array}{rr}
8 & 7 \\
- \ 5 & 3 \\
\hline
\end{array}
$$

You can subtract 3-digit numbers by lining up the digits.

Example: 256 − 124

Write hundreds under hundreds. Write tens under tens. Write ones under ones.

Subtract ones. Subtract tens. Subtract hundreds.

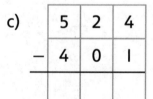

---

5. Subtract. Start in the ones place.

a)
	7	2	9
−	3	1	6

b)
	8	9	5
−	2	5	4

c)
	5	2	4
−	4	0	1

d)
	3	9	8
−	1	6	3

e)
	5	2	3
−	3	1	0

f)
	9	5	8
−	4	2	3

g)
	4	6	4
−	2	6	1

h)
	3	7	8
−	3	6	1

COPYRIGHT © JUMP MATH: NOT TO BE COPIED. US EDITION

8. Subtraction with Regrouping—Tens

I. Regroup I tens block as 10 ones blocks.

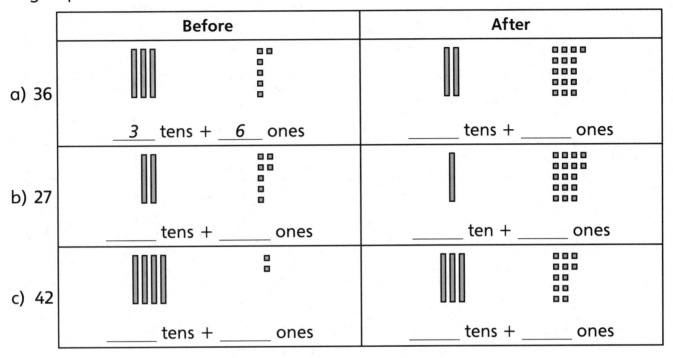

	Before	After
a) 36	_3_ tens + _6_ ones	_____ tens + _____ ones
b) 27	_____ tens + _____ ones	_____ ten + _____ ones
c) 42	_____ tens + _____ ones	_____ tens + _____ ones

2. Regroup I ten as 10 ones.

a)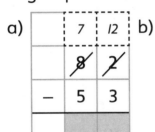

	7	12
	8̸	2̸
−	5	3

b)
6	1
− 4	8

c)
4	0
− 1	9

d)
5	1
− 4	7

e)
3	5
− 1	8

f)
5	0
− 3	6

g)
9	5
− 2	8

h)
2	8
− 1	9

i)
3	3
− 2	5

j)
7	4
− 4	6

k)
4	2
− 2	7

l)
8	3
− 3	8

m)
6	1
− 5	7

n)
9	0
− 8	9

o)
5	8
− 3	9

COPYRIGHT © JUMP MATH: NOT TO BE COPIED. US EDITION

3. Regroup I ten as 10 ones. Then subtract. Start in the ones place.

a)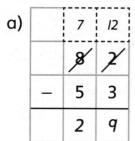

b)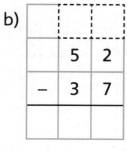

c)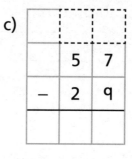

d)

	8	1
−	5	7

e)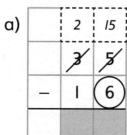

f)

	8	7
−	3	8

g)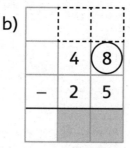

h)

	6	6
−	2	8

4. Circle the greater digit in the ones place. If you need to regroup, write "regroup." If you do not need to regroup, write "OK."

a) 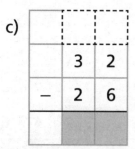 <u>regroup</u>

5 is less than 6

b)  <u>OK</u>

c) 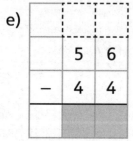 _____

d)

	5	8
−	2	7

_____

e)

	5	6
−	4	4

_____

f) 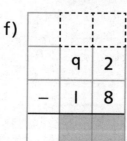 _____

COPYRIGHT © JUMP MATH: NOT TO BE COPIED. US EDITION

5. Write "regroup" or "OK." Then subtract, regrouping if needed.

a)

	2	15
	3̸	5̸
−	1	6
	1	9

__regroup__

5 is less than 6

b)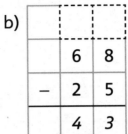

	6	8
−	2	5
	4	3

__OK__

c)

	3	2
−	2	6

_____

d)

	4	8
−	2	7

_____

6. Subtract. Regroup if needed.

a)

	3	12
	4̸	2̸
−	2	7
	1	5

b)

	5	2
−	3	1

c)

	6	6
−	2	9

d)

	8	1
−	5	0

e)

	4	4
−	3	7

f)

	9	7
−	3	9

g)

	4	4
−	2	4

h)

	5	6
−	1	5

i)

	9	2
−	8	1

j)

	8	7
−	3	7

k)

	5	0
−	1	7

l)

	9	2
−	2	6

7. Do you need to regroup the top number in this question? Explain.

```
   62
 − 47
 _____
```

COPYRIGHT © JUMP MATH: NOT TO BE COPIED. US EDITION

9. Subtraction with Regrouping—Hundreds

To subtract 327 – 182, regroup 1 hundreds block as 10 tens blocks.

Then subtract by crossing out ones, tens, and hundreds.

Hundreds	Tens	Ones
3	2	7

Hundreds	Tens	Ones
2	12	7

Hundreds	Tens	Ones
1	4	5

1. Regroup 1 hundred as 10 tens.

a)
```
      7  12
      8  2  4
   -  5  3  3
```

b)
```
      5  6  9
   -  3  8  8
```

c)
```
      2  4  8
   -  1  5  7
```

d)
```
      5  3  8
   -  2  4  6
```

2. Regroup 1 hundred as 10 tens. Then subtract. Start in the ones place.

a)
```
      3  15
      4  5  4
   -  2  6  3
```

b)
```
      4  6  7
   -  3  8  5
```

c)
```
      3  5  8
   -  1  6  7
```

d)
```
      9  3  6
   -  2  7  6
```

e)
```
      2  5  2
   -  1  9  0
```

f)
```
      8  8  5
   -  3  9  2
```

g)
```
      5  2  6
   -  3  8  4
```

h)
```
      4  3  3
   -  2  8  2
```

COPYRIGHT © JUMP MATH: NOT TO BE COPIED. US EDITION

3. Subtract. Regroup I hundred as 10 tens, or I ten as 10 ones.

a)
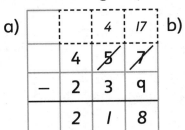

		4	17
	4	5̸	7̸
−	2	3	9
	2	1	8

b)

	3	6	6
−	2	9	5

c)

	4	6	6
−	1	3	9

d)

	8	2	5
−	2	7	4

e)
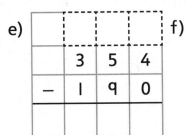

	3	5	4
−	1	9	0

f)

	2	8	4
−	1	9	2

g)

	6	9	6
−	3	8	8

h)

	4	1	7
−	2	8	2

i)

	5	6	7
−	2	9	3

j)

	4	5	1
−	3	2	7

k)

	6	4	8
−	3	5	1

l)

	2	7	8
−	1	6	9

To subtract 642 − 279, you need to regroup twice.

Step 1:

		3	12
	6	4̸	2̸
−	2	7	9

Step 2:

		3	12
	6	4̸	2̸
−	2	7	9
			3

Step 3:

		13	
	5	3̸	12
	6̸	4̸	2̸
−	2	7	9
			3

Step 4:

		13	
	5	3̸	12
	6̸	4̸	2̸
−	2	7	9
		6	3

Step 5:

		13	
	5	3̸	12
	6̸	4̸	2̸
−	2	7	9
	3	6	3

4. Subtract. You will need to regroup twice.

a)

	4	5	7
−	2	6	9

b)

	4	6	7
−	1	9	8

c)
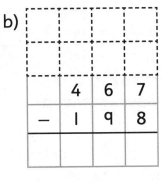

	3	2	1
−	1	6	7

d)
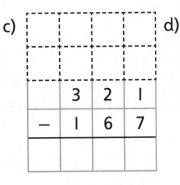

	9	3	6
−	2	7	8

COPYRIGHT © JUMP MATH: NOT TO BE COPIED. US EDITION

5. Subtract. You will need to regroup twice.

a)
```
    3   2   7
-   1   6   9
```

b)
```
    5   8   7
-   1   9   8
```

c)
```
    8   1   1
-   2   7   5
```

d)
```
    7   2   5
-   2   7   8
```

e)
```
    2   5   2
-   1   9   9
```

f)
```
    4   7   5
-   2   9   6
```

g)
```
    8   2   5
-   3   3   6
```

h)
```
    4   4   4
-   2   8   8
```

6. Subtract. Regroup when needed.

a)
```
    4   3   7
-   1   0   9
```

b)
```
    4   8   7
-   1   9   2
```

c)
```
    4   2   1
-   1   7   7
```

d)
```
    7   2   5
-   2   1   3
```

e)
```
    3   6   3
-   1   9   9
```

f)
```
    4   2   2
-   2   9   6
```

g)
```
    8   2   5
-   3   1   3
```

h)
```
    4   4   4
-   2   8   1
```

7. Sam has 346 dollars. He gives 175 dollars to a charity. How much money does he have left? Show your work.

8. Clara has 562 stickers in her collection. She gives 384 stickers to her sister. How many stickers does Clara have left?

COPYRIGHT © JUMP MATH: NOT TO BE COPIED. US EDITION

To subtract from 100, you need to regroup from the hundreds before you can regroup from the tens. Example:

Step 1:

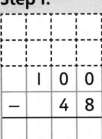

Step 2:

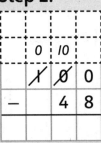

Step 3:

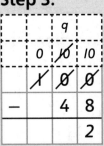

Step 4:

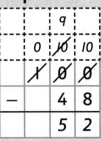

9. Subtract by regrouping.

a)

	1	0	0
−		4	7

b)

	1	0	0
−		5	2

c)

	1	0	0
−		6	5

d)

	1	0	0
−		1	9

10. Now subtract from 99 without regrouping.

a)

	9	9
−	4	7

b)

	9	9
−	5	2

c)

	9	9
−	6	5

d)

	9	9
−	1	9

To subtract from 100, first subtract from 99. Then add 1 to your answer.

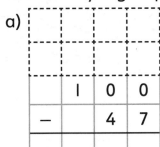

11. Subtract from 99. Use the answer to subtract from 100.

a)

	9	9
−	4	7

$100 - 47 = \underline{\hspace{1cm}}$

b)

	9	9
−	3	2

$100 - 32 = \underline{\hspace{1cm}}$

c)

	9	9
−	5	6

$100 - 56 = \underline{\hspace{1cm}}$

d)

	9	9
−	2	7

$100 - 27 = \underline{\hspace{1cm}}$

COPYRIGHT © JUMP MATH: NOT TO BE COPIED. US EDITION

10. Puzzles and Problems

1. Tasha has 12 colored pencils. 8 are at home and the rest are at school.

    a) How many pencil crayons are at school?

    b) How did you solve the problem? (Did you use a calculation? Make a model? Draw a picture?)

2. The Statue of Liberty in New York is 305 feet tall. The Spring Temple Buddha in Henan, China, is 420 feet tall.

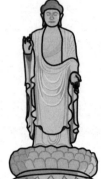

    a) Which statue is taller? How do you know?

    b) How much taller is the taller statue?

3. Rani wants to add the numbers. She starts by adding the ones digits. Explain why Rani wrote the number 1 above the 3.

a)

	1	
	3	5
+	4	9
		4

b)

	1		
	3	6	7
+	2	4	1
		0	8

4. Find the mistake in Ben's work.

a)

	2	
	4	7
+	2	5
	8	1

b)

	3	9
+	5	
	8	9

c)

	1		
	5	8	
+	2	6	0
	8	4	0

5. Jin has 17 books. Tina has 35 books.

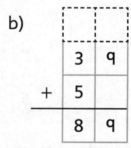

    a) How many more books does Tina have than Jin?

    b) How many books do they have altogether?

COPYRIGHT © JUMP MATH: NOT TO BE COPIED. US EDITION

6. Sandy has 243 marbles. Tony has 178 marbles.

    a) How many marbles do they have in total?

    b) How do you know that Sandy has more marbles than Tony?

    c) How many more marbles does Sandy have? Show your work.

7. Find the mistake in Glen's work.

a)

	_16_
5	6
− 4	8
1	8

b)

5	6	3
− 2	4	
3	2	3

c)

	_3_	_14_
	~~4~~	~~3~~
	− 2	8
	1	6

8. Pens cost 53 cents. Erasers cost 44 cents. Ethan has 98 cents.

    a) Does he have enough money to buy a pen and an eraser?

    b) Explain how you know.

9. Place the numbers 1, 2, 3, 4 in the top four boxes to make the largest possible sum.

10. Place the numbers 1, 2, 3, 4 in the top four boxes to make the largest possible difference.

11. Here are the heights of some American monuments.

    a) Write the heights in order from least to greatest.

    b) How much taller is the Washington Monument than the Statue of Liberty?

    c) How much taller is the tallest structure than the shortest?

Heights of Monuments	
Crazy Horse Memorial	564 feet
Statue of Liberty	305 feet
Washington Monument	554 feet

COPYRIGHT © JUMP MATH: NOT TO BE COPIED. US EDITION

11. Mental Math

1. Fill in the missing numbers.

a) $7 = \boxed{1} + \boxed{}$
$\boxed{2} + \boxed{}$
$\boxed{3} + \boxed{}$

b) $6 = \boxed{1} + \boxed{}$
$\boxed{2} + \boxed{}$
$\boxed{3} + \boxed{}$

2. Fill in the missing numbers.

$10 = \boxed{1} + \boxed{}$
$\boxed{2} + \boxed{}$
$\boxed{3} + \boxed{}$
$\boxed{4} + \boxed{}$
$\boxed{5} + \boxed{}$

3. Circle the pair that adds to 10.

a) ②   7   ⑧

b) 3   7   4

c) 5   3   5

d) 6   4   5

e) 1   8   9

4. Circle the pair that adds to 10. Write the number that is left over in the box.

a) ④ + 5 + ⑥ = 10 + $\boxed{5}$

b) $7 + 3 + 4 = 10 + \boxed{}$

c) $8 + 3 + 2 = 10 + \boxed{}$

d) $6 + 9 + 4 = 10 + \boxed{}$

e) $9 + 1 + 7 = 10 + \boxed{}$

f) $5 + 8 + 2 = 10 + \boxed{}$

g) $5 + 3 + 5 = 10 + \boxed{}$

h) $3 + 9 + 1 = 10 + \boxed{}$

i) $3 + 7 + 4 = 10 + \boxed{}$

j) $6 + 5 + 4 = 10 + \boxed{}$

k) $5 + 7 + 5 = 10 + \boxed{}$

l) $5 + 7 + 3 = 10 + \boxed{}$

m) $3 + 7 + 8 = 10 + \boxed{}$

n) $4 + 8 + 6 = 10 + \boxed{}$

COPYRIGHT © JUMP MATH: NOT TO BE COPIED. US EDITION

5. Add mentally.

a) 10 + 5 = _____

b) 10 + 7 = _____

c) 40 + 8 = _____

d) 50 + 9 = _____

e) 60 + 1 = _____

f) 20 + 3 = _____

g) 40 + 4 = _____

h) 30 + 6 = _____

i) 90 + 9 = _____

j) 120 + 5 = _____

k) 460 + 7 = _____

l) 980 + 6 = _____

m) 800 + 3 = _____

n) 670 + 5 = _____

BONUS ▶

o) 400 + 12 = _____

p) 300 + 25 = _____

6. Fill in the boxes.

a) 8 + 6 = 8 + ⟨2⟩ + ⟨4⟩

these make 10   left over

b) 9 + 5 = 9 + ☐ + ☐

these make 10   left over

c) 6 + 5 = 6 + ☐ + ☐

these make 10   left over

d) 5 + 7 = 5 + ☐ + ☐

these make 10   left over

e) 9 + 4 = 9 + ☐ + ☐

f) 8 + 8 = 8 + ☐ + ☐

g) 7 + 6 = 7 + ☐ + ☐

h) 9 + 6 = 9 + ☐ + ☐

i) 6 + 6 = 6 + ☐ + ☐

j) 8 + 7 = 8 + ☐ + ☐

k) 7 + 8 = 7 + ☐ + ☐

l) 5 + 8 = 5 + ☐ + ☐

m) 6 + 9 = 6 + ☐ + ☐

n) 8 + 3 = 8 + ☐ + ☐

COPYRIGHT © JUMP MATH: NOT TO BE COPIED. US EDITION

7. Add by following the steps.

a) $7 + 5 = \boxed{7} + \boxed{3} + \boxed{2} = \underline{\ 10 + 2 = 12\ }$

these make 10   left over

b) $26 + 5 = 26 + \boxed{} + \boxed{} = \underline{\hspace{3cm}}$

these make 30   left over

c) $78 + 6 = 78 + \boxed{} + \boxed{} = \underline{\hspace{3cm}}$

these make 80   left over

d) $45 + 8 = 45 + \boxed{} + \boxed{} = \underline{\hspace{3cm}}$

these make 50   left over

e) $37 + 8 = 37 + \boxed{} + \boxed{} = \underline{\hspace{3cm}}$

these make ____   left over

f) $68 + 7 = 68 + \boxed{} + \boxed{} = \underline{\hspace{3cm}}$

these make ____   left over

8. Find the answers mentally.

a) Roy has 38 dollars.
His parents give him 7 dollars.
How much money does Roy have?

b) Don has 26 stickers.
Emma has 7 stickers.
How many do they have altogether?

9. Explain how you would add 37 + 5 mentally.

10. Add 48 + 5 mentally. Then use your answer to add 480 + 50 mentally.

COPYRIGHT © JUMP MATH: NOT TO BE COPIED. US EDITION

12. Parts and Totals

I. Shade boxes to show the number of marbles. Then find the total and the difference.

a) 5 green marbles
   3 blue marbles

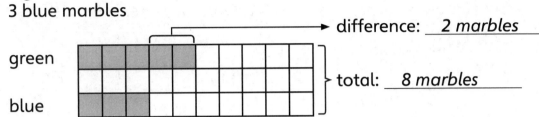

difference: _2 marbles_

total: _8 marbles_

b) 4 green marbles
   6 blue marbles

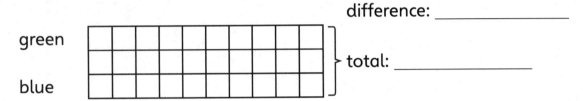

difference: _____

total: _____

c) 8 green marbles
   4 blue marbles

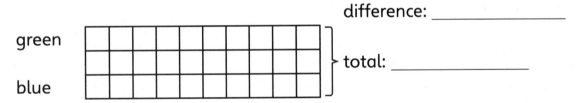

difference: _____

total: _____

d) 9 green marbles
   4 blue marbles

difference: _____

total: _____

e) 3 green marbles
   8 blue marbles

difference: _____

total: _____

COPYRIGHT © JUMP MATH: NOT TO BE COPIED. US EDITION

4 green marbles
3 more blue marbles than green

To draw the diagram:

Step I: Shade the amount you know.   **Step 2:** Find the other amount.

green   [grid]   green   [grid]

blue   [grid]

2. Draw the diagram. Then fill in the blanks.

a) 5 green marbles
   2 more blue marbles than green marbles

   difference: _____

   green   [grid]

   blue   } total: _____

b) 4 blue marbles
   3 more green marbles than blue marbles

   difference: _____

   green   [grid]

   blue   } total: _____

Sometimes you know the larger amount.

   6 green marbles   4 more green marbles than blue marbles

   green   [grid]   green   [grid]

                            blue   [grid]

3. Draw the diagram. Then fill in the blanks.

   7 green marbles
   3 more green marbles than blue marbles

                            difference: _____

   green   [grid]

   blue   } total: _____

COPYRIGHT © JUMP MATH: NOT TO BE COPIED. US EDITION

4. Draw the diagram. Then fill in the blanks.

a) 9 green marbles
   5 blue marbles

difference: _____

total: _____

b) 6 marbles altogether
   2 green marbles

difference: _____

total: _____

c) 3 green marbles
   4 more blue marbles than green marbles

difference: _____

total: _____

d) 8 green marbles
   3 fewer blue marbles than green marbles

difference: _____

total: _____

e) 9 blue marbles
   15 marbles altogether

difference: _____

total: _____

COPYRIGHT © JUMP MATH: NOT TO BE COPIED. US EDITION

13. More Parts and Totals

1. Fill in the table.

	Green Marbles	Blue Marbles	Total	Difference
a)	3	5	8	*2 more blue marbles than green*
b)	2	9		
c)	4		6	
d)		2	7	
e)	6		10	
f)	3			1 more blue marble than green
g)		2		1 more green marble than blue
h)		4		1 more blue marble than green
i)	7	2		5 more green marbles than blue
j)		5		4 more green marbles than blue
k)		12		6 more blue marbles than green
l)	12	35		
m)	35			20 more green marbles than blue

COPYRIGHT © JUMP MATH: NOT TO BE COPIED. US EDITION

2. Write + or −.

a)
| Number of green marbles | ◯ | Number of blue marbles | = | Total number of marbles |

b)
| Number of green marbles | ◯ | Number of blue marbles | = | How many more green marbles |

c)
| Number of green apples | ◯ | Number of red apples | = | Total number of apples |

d)
| Total number of apples | ◯ | Number of red apples | = | Number of green apples |

e)
| Number of green grapes | ◯ | Number of purple grapes | = | How many more green grapes |

f)
| Number of yellow beans | ◯ | Number of green beans | = | How many more yellow beans |

g)
| Total number of beans | ◯ | Number of yellow beans | = | Number of green beans |

h)
| Number of red marbles | ◯ | Number of blue marbles | = | How many more red marbles |

COPYRIGHT © JUMP MATH: NOT TO BE COPIED. US EDITION

3. Fill in the table. Circle the number in the table that answers the question.

		Red	Green	Total	Difference
a)	Kate has 3 green fish and 4 red fish. How many fish does she have altogether?	4	3	⑦	1
b)	Bill has 4 green fish and 6 red fish. How many fish does he have altogether?				
c)	Mary has 8 green fish and 2 more green fish than red fish. How many fish does she have?				
d)	Peter has 19 fish. He has 15 green fish. How many red fish does he have?				
e)	Hanna has 8 green fish and 3 fewer red fish than green fish. How many fish does she have?				
f)	Ken has 22 red fish and 33 green fish. How many more green fish does he have?				

4. Alice has 3 science books and 4 art books. How many books does she have?

5. Marco has 5 pets. 3 are cats. The rest are dogs. How many dogs does he have?

6. Ed has 25 red apples. He has 14 more green apples than red apples. How many apples does he have?

7. There are 25 students in a class. 16 of the students are girls.

   a) How many students are boys?

   b) How many more girls are there than boys?

COPYRIGHT © JUMP MATH: NOT TO BE COPIED. US EDITION

14. Sums and Differences

1. Micky has 7 dollars and Amy has 15 dollars. How much money do they have altogether?

2. Anne is 12 years old. Her sister is 23. How much older is her sister?

3. A library has 520 books. 150 were borrowed. How many books are left?

4. 52 students went on a school trip. 27 of the students were girls. How many were boys?

5. Jayden paid 75 cents for a goldfish that costs 62 cents. How much change did he get back?

6. Clara's mother is 47. Her aunt is 33. How much older is Clara's mother than Clara's aunt?

7. A pine tree is 53 feet tall. An oak tree is 75 feet tall. How much taller is the oak tree than the pine tree?

8. Ethan sold 27 raffle tickets altogether on Wednesday and Thursday. On Thursday, he sold 13 tickets. How many tickets did he sell on Wednesday?

9. Sara had 35 colored pencils. She lost 4. How many does she have left?

COPYRIGHT © JUMP MATH: NOT TO BE COPIED. US EDITION

10. The biggest woolly mammoth tusk ever found weighs 208 pounds. How much would 2 tusks of this size weigh?

11. Beth biked 15 miles on Monday and 12 miles on Tuesday.

   a) How much farther did she bike on Monday than on Tuesday?

   b) How far did she bike altogether?

12. Ravi hiked 9 miles on Tuesday. He hiked 4 more miles on Wednesday than on Tuesday.

   a) How far did he hike on Wednesday?

   b) How far did he hike altogether?

13. Zack has 42 cents. Nina has 15 cents more than Zack. How much money do they have altogether?

14. Josh read two books by Roald Dahl. *The BFG* is 208 pages long. *Charlie and the Chocolate Factory* is 53 pages shorter than *The BFG*. How many pages did he read altogether?

15. Marta bought 29 baseball cards and 16 football cards. She gave away 2 baseball cards and 3 football cards. How many cards does she have left?

COPYRIGHT © JUMP MATH: NOT TO BE COPIED. US EDITION

15. Even and Odd Numbers

> The number of dots is **even** if you can pair all the dots.
>
> The number of dots is **odd** if you cannot pair all the dots.

1. Circle two dots at a time. Then write "even" or "odd."

a)

7 is ___odd___

b)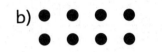

8 is _____

c)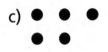

5 is _____

d)

6 is _____

e)

9 is _____

f)

10 is _____

> Even numbers are the numbers you say when you count by 2s starting from 0:
>
> 0, 2, 4, 6, 8, and so on. Zero is an even number.

2. a) Underline the ones digit of the even numbers.

1	2	3	4	5	6	7	8	9	10
11	12	13	14	15	16	17	18	19	20
21	22	23	24	25	26	27	28	29	30
31	32	33	34	35	36	37	38	39	40

b) What pattern do you see in the ones digits of the even numbers?
Write the pattern.

___2___ , ___4___ , _____, _____, _____, _____, _____, _____, _____, _____

3. Use the pattern you found to fill in the blanks.

a) 46, 48, 50, ___52___ , _____, _____

b) 76, 78, 80, _____, _____, _____

c) 52, 54, 56, _____, _____, _____

d) 82, 84, 86, _____, _____, _____

COPYRIGHT © JUMP MATH: NOT TO BE COPIED. US EDITION

Odd numbers are the numbers that are not even: 1, 3, 5, 7, 9, and so on.

4. a) Underline the ones digit of the odd numbers.

1	2	3	4	5	6	7	8	9	10
11	12	13	14	15	16	17	18	19	20
21	22	23	24	25	26	27	28	29	30
31	32	33	34	35	36	37	38	39	40

b) What pattern do you see in the ones digits of the odd numbers? Write the pattern.

____1____ , ___3___ , _____ , _____ , _____ , _____ , _____ , _____ , _____ , _____ , _____ , _____

5. Use the pattern you found to fill in the blanks.

a) 47, 49, 51, ___53___ , _____, _____

b) 67, 69, 71, _____, _____, _____

c) 53, 55, 57, _____, _____, _____

d) 81, 83, 85, _____, _____, _____

6. Fill in the missing even or odd numbers.

a) 22, ___24___ , _____, 28

b) 29, 31, _____, 35

c) _____, 92, 94, _____

d) _____, 67, 69, _____

e) _____, 39, _____, 43

f) _____, 40, _____, 44

7. Add. Is the answer even or odd?

a) 7 + 3 = ___10___ , ___even___

b) 4 + 8 = _____, _____

c) 2 + 9 = _____, _____

d) 5 + 4 = _____, _____

e) 6 + 2 = _____, _____

f) 1 + 4 = _____, _____

8. If you add two even numbers, will the sum be odd or even? Explain.

COPYRIGHT © JUMP MATH: NOT TO BE COPIED. US EDITION

16. Adding a Sequence of Numbers

You can add a **sequence** of numbers by keeping track of the sums.

 $\xrightarrow{\text{add } 2 + 2 = 4}$ $\xrightarrow{\text{add } 4 + 2 = 6}$

2 + 2 + 2 = _____   2 + 2 + 2 = _____   2 + 2 + 2 = __6__

I. Add the numbers. Use boxes to keep track of the sums.

        (box with 6)   (empty box)   (empty box)

a) 3 + 3 + 3 = __9__   b) 4 + 4 + 4 = _____   c) 6 + 6 + 6 = _____

d) 3 + 3 + 3 + 3 = _____   e) 4 + 4 + 4 + 4 = _____   f) 5 + 5 + 5 + 5 = _____

(two empty boxes)   (two empty boxes)   (one empty box)

g) 2 + 2 + 2 + 2 = _____   h) 6 + 6 + 6 + 6 = _____   i) 5 + 5 + 5 = _____

2. Write an addition sentence for the picture. Add to find the number of apples.

a) 2 apples in each box   3 boxes

     2 + 2 + 2 = 6 apples

b) 3 apples in each box   4 boxes

_____

c) 4 apples in each box   2 boxes

_____

d) 3 apples in each box   3 boxes

_____

e) 5 apples in each box   4 boxes

_____

f) 6 apples in each box   2 boxes

_____

COPYRIGHT © JUMP MATH: NOT TO BE COPIED. US EDITION

3. Draw a picture and write an addition sentence for your picture.

a) 2 boats

   3 kids in each boat

_____

b) 4 plates

   2 apples on each plate

_____

c) 3 boxes

   5 pencils in each box

_____

d) 3 fish bowls

   2 fish in each bowl

_____

4. Write an addition sentence.

a) 4 boxes   3 flowers in each box

_____

b) 6 wagons   3 kids in each wagon

_____

c) 5 bags   I banana in each bag

_____

d) 5 baskets   6 oranges in each basket

_____

e) 4 boats   8 kids in each boat

_____

f) 2 vans   9 people in each van

_____

BONUS ▶ Yu sees some boxes of apples at a store. She writes a sentence
for the total number of apples: $75 + 75 + 75 + 75 = 300$.

a) How many apples are in each box? _____

b) How many boxes of apples does Yu see? _____

COPYRIGHT © JUMP MATH: NOT TO BE COPIED. US EDITION

17. Skip Counting by 2s and 4s

You can **skip count** by 2s starting at 0. Add 2 each time.

$$0 \xrightarrow{+2} 2 \xrightarrow{+2} 4 \xrightarrow{+2} 6 \xrightarrow{+2} 8 \xrightarrow{+2} 10$$

I. Skip count by 2s.

a) 12, 14, 16, _____, _____, _____

b) 42, 44, 46, _____, _____, _____

c) 68, 70, 72, _____, _____, _____

d) 80, 82, 84, _____, _____, _____

e) 54, 56, 58, _____, _____, _____

f) 88, 90, 92, _____, _____, _____

2. Add. Use skip counting to keep track of the sum.

a) 2 + 2 + 2 = _____

b) 2 + 2 + 2 + 2 = _____

c) 2 + 2 + 2 + 2 + 2 + 2 + 2 = _____

You can skip count by 4s starting at 0. Add 4 each time.

$$0 \xrightarrow{+4} 4 \xrightarrow{+4} 8 \xrightarrow{+4} 12 \xrightarrow{+4} 16 \xrightarrow{+4} 20$$

3. Continue the sequence.

a) 4 , 8 , 12 , _____, _____, _____

b) 20 , 24 , 28 , _____, _____, _____

You can skip count by 4s a different way:
* Skip count by 2s.
* Circle every second number.   ⓪, 2 ,④, 6 ,⑧

4. Use the new way to skip count by 4s.

⑧, 10 , 12 , 14 , 16 , 18 , 20 , _____, _____, _____, _____, _____, _____, _____, _____

COPYRIGHT © JUMP MATH: NOT TO BE COPIED. US EDITION

5. The chart shows the numbers you say when skip counting by 4s. The first two numbers have 0s added.

04	08	12	16	20
24	28	32	36	40

Describe any patterns you see in the **columns** of the chart.

_____

_____

_____

6. Find the sums by skip counting by 4s.

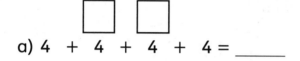

a) 4 + 4 + 4 + 4 = _____

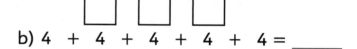

b) 4 + 4 + 4 + 4 + 4 = _____

7. Ben skip counted by 2s or 4s. Fill in the missing numbers. Then write the number he counted by.

a) | 8 | 10 | ☐ | 14 |

He counted by _____.

b) | 8 | ☐ | 16 | ☐ |

He counted by _____.

c) | 16 | ☐ | ☐ | 22 |

He counted by _____.

d) | 24 | ☐ | ☐ | 36 |

He counted by _____.

8. Are the numbers you say when skip counting by 4s all even? YES NO Explain.

_____

_____

_____

COPYRIGHT © JUMP MATH: NOT TO BE COPIED. US EDITION

18. Skip Counting by 5s and 10s

1. Underline the ones digit of the numbers you say when skip counting by 5s.

    a) <u>5</u> , 1<u>0</u> , 15 , 20 , 25 , 30

    Pattern in the ones digits: 5 , 0 , _____, _____, _____, _____

    b) 35 , 40 , 45 , 50 , 55 , 60 , 65

    Pattern in the ones digits: _____, _____, _____, _____, _____, _____, _____

2. Circle the numbers you say when skip counting by 5s.

    17   15   23   42   75   92   80   85   33   95   14

3. Jen skip counted by 10s.

    a) Continue the sequence.

    0 , 10 , 20 , _____, _____, _____, _____, _____, _____, _____

    b) Describe any patterns you see in the ones and tens digits of the sequence.

    _____

4. Find the amount of money by skip counting.

    a)   b)

    5, 10, _____, _____, _____, _____   10, 20, _____, _____, _____, _____

    c)   d)

    _____, _____, _____, _____, _____   _____, _____, _____, _____

5. A book costs 5 dollars. Alex buys 6 books. Use skip counting to find out how much he spent.

    _____   _____   _____   _____   _____   _____
    1 book   2 books   3 books   4 books   5 books   6 books

6. Explain how you knew which numbers to circle in Question 2.

COPYRIGHT © JUMP MATH: NOT TO BE COPIED. US EDITION

19. Skip Counting by 3s and 6s

1. Continue the sequence by skip counting by 3s.

0 , 3 , 6 , 9 , _____, _____, _____, _____, _____, _____

2. Add the numbers. Use skip counting to keep track of the sums.

a) ☐ ☐

3 + 3 + 3 + 3 = _____

b) ☐ ☐ ☐ ☐

3 + 3 + 3 + 3 + 3 + 3 = _____

3. Skip count by 3s.

a) wheels on tricycles

__3__ , __6__ , _____

b) sides of triangles

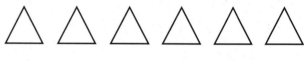

__3__ , __6__ , _____, _____, _____, _____

> You say the multiples of 3 when you skip count by 3s.
>
> 0, 3, 6, 9, 12, and so on are **multiples of 3**.

4. The chart shows some multiples of 3. The first three numbers have 0s added.

03	06	09
12	15	18
21	24	27

Describe any patterns you see in the columns.
Hint: Look at the ones digits and the tens digits.

_____

_____

_____

COPYRIGHT © JUMP MATH: NOT TO BE COPIED. US EDITION

You can skip count by 6s.
- Skip count by 3s.
- Circle every second number.   ⓪, 3 ,⑥, 9 , ⑫

5. Skip count by 6s to 30.

⓪, 3 ,⑥, _____, _____, _____, _____, _____, _____, _____, _____

6. Add the numbers. Use skip counting to keep track of the sums.

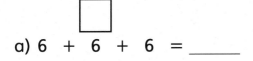   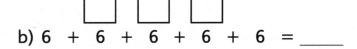

a) 6 + 6 + 6 = _____   b) 6 + 6 + 6 + 6 + 6 = _____

7. Helen skip counted by 2s, 3s, 4s, or 5s. Fill in the missing numbers.
Write the number she counted by.

a)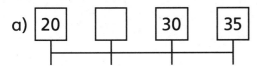

She counted by _____.

b) | 4 | | 8 |

She counted by _____.

c)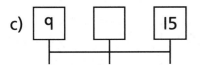

She counted by _____.

d)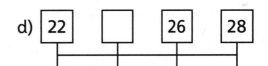

She counted by _____.

e)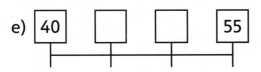

She counted by _____.

f)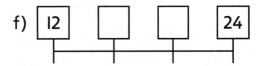

She counted by _____.

8. Are all multiples of 3 odd numbers?   YES   NO   Explain.

_____

_____

_____

COPYRIGHT © JUMP MATH: NOT TO BE COPIED. US EDITION

20. Multiplication and Repeated Addition

We use **multiplication** as a short way to write addition of the same number.

$$4 \times 3 = \underbrace{3 + 3 + 3 + 3}_{\text{add 3 four times}}$$

This is **repeated addition.**

I. Complete the number sentence using repeated addition.

a) $4 \times 2 = $ ___$2 + 2 + 2 + 2$___

b) $3 \times 2 = $ _____

c) $3 \times 4 = $ _____

d) $4 \times 5 = $ _____

e) $2 \times 3 = $ _____

f) $1 \times 5 = $ _____

g) $5 \times 2 = $ _____

h) $3 \times 5 = $ _____

2. Complete the number sentence using multiplication.

a) $2 + 2 + 2 = $ ___3×2___

b) $4 + 4 = $ _____

c) $6 + 6 + 6 = $ _____

d) $3 + 3 + 3 = $ _____

e) $9 + 9 + 9 = $ _____

f) $7 + 7 + 7 + 7 + 7 = $ _____

g) $8 + 8 + 8 + 8 = $ _____

h) $5 + 5 + 5 + 5 + 5 + 5 = $ _____

i) $4 + 4 + 4 + 4 = $ _____

j) $1 + 1 + 1 = $ _____

3. Circle the additions that cannot be written as multiplications.

$2 + 2 + 2 + 2$	$3 + 4 + 3 + 3 + 3$	$2 + 5 + 7$	$7 + 7 + 7 + 7$
$4 + 4 + 4 + 4 + 4$	$9 + 9 + 9 + 9 + 9$	$5 + 5 + 5 + 8$	$6 + 6 + 6$
$17 + 17 + 17$	$101 + 101 + 101$	$4 + 4 + 9 + 4$	$3 + 3$

COPYRIGHT © JUMP MATH: NOT TO BE COPIED. US EDITION

4. Write an addition sentence. Then write a multiplication sentence.

a) 3 boxes

2 pencils in each box

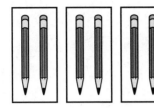

$\underline{\ \ 2 + 2 + 2 = 6\ \ }$

$\underline{\ \ 3 \times 2 = 6\ \ }$

b) 4 boxes

5 pencils in each box

_____

_____

c) 2 boxes

4 pencils in each box

_____

_____

d) 3 boxes

3 pencils in each box

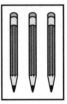

_____

_____

5. Write a multiplication sentence.

a) 3 boxes

4 plums in each box

$\underline{\ \ 3 \times 4 = 12\ \ }$

b) 4 boxes

6 apples in each box

_____

c) 3 boxes

5 bananas in each box

_____

d) 5 boxes

10 crayons in each box

_____

BONUS ▶ Complete the number sentence using multiplication.

$100 + 100 + 100 + 100 + 100 + 100 + 100 + 100 + 100 =$ _____

COPYRIGHT © JUMP MATH: NOT TO BE COPIED. US EDITION

21. Multiplication and Equal Groups

Show **equal groups** of objects.
- Use circles for the groups.
- Use dots for the objects.

4 groups of 3

I. Write what the picture shows.

a)

_____ groups of _____

b)

_____ groups of _____

2. Draw equal groups. Use circles for the groups and dots for the objects.

a) 4 groups of 2

b) 3 groups of 4

3. Write an addition sentence for the picture. Then write a multiplication sentence.

a)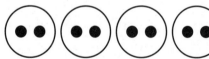

___4___ groups of ___2___

___2 + 2 + 2 + 2___ = _____

___4 × 2___ = _____

b)

_____ groups of _____

_____ = _____

_____ = _____

c)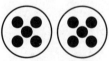

_____ groups of _____

_____ = _____

_____ = _____

d)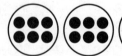

_____ groups of _____

_____ = _____

_____ = _____

COPYRIGHT © JUMP MATH: NOT TO BE COPIED. US EDITION

4. Draw a picture. Then write a multiplication sentence. Find the total number of dots.

a) 3 groups of 5

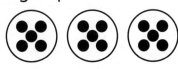

_____ circles

_____ dots in a circle

_3 × 5 = 15_____

b) 2 groups of 6

_____ circles

_____ dots in a circle

_____

c) 5 groups of 4

_____ circles

_____ dots in a circle

_____

d) 6 groups of 3

_____ circles

_____ dots in a circle

_____

e) 2 groups of 4

_____ circles

_____ dots in a circle

_____

f) 3 groups of 3

_____ circles

_____ dots in a circle

_____

5. A canoe can hold 3 children. How many children can 4 canoes hold?

6. Ravi needs lemons for his lemonade stand. He buys 3 bags with 6 lemons in each bag. How many lemons did he buy in total?

7. Ava is planning a soccer tournament. She has 4 teams with 6 players on each team. How many players are there in total?

COPYRIGHT © JUMP MATH: NOT TO BE COPIED. US EDITION

22. Doubles

1. Double each number.

   a) Double 3 is ___6___.

   b) Double 4 is ___8___.

   c) Double 6 is _____.

   d) Double 2 is _____.

   e) Double 7 is _____.

   f) Double 8 is _____.

2. Double the ones digit. Then double the tens digit to get double the number.

   a)

Number	24	14	12	32	34	22
Double	48					

   b)

Number	82	51	64	54	92	74
Double						

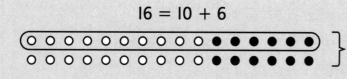

$16 = 10 + 6$

So double 16 is $20 + 12$

double 10   double 6

3.

	17	15	25	37	48
Write the tens and ones	10 + 7				
Double the tens and ones	20 + 14				
Double	34				

4. Double 3 times the number to find 6 times the number.

   a) $3 \times 2 =$ _____

   so $6 \times 2 =$ _____

   b) $3 \times 4 =$ _____

   so $6 \times 4 =$ _____

   c) $3 \times 8 =$ _____

   so $6 \times 8 =$ _____

   d) $3 \times 5 =$ _____

   so $6 \times 5 =$ _____

   e) $3 \times 6 =$ _____

   so $6 \times 6 =$ _____

   f) $3 \times 9 =$ _____

   so $6 \times 9 =$ _____

COPYRIGHT © JUMP MATH: NOT TO BE COPIED. US EDITION

5. Use doubles to find the products.

a)

If	$2 \times 7 = 14$	$3 \times 7 = 21$	$4 \times 7 = 28$	$2 \times 6 = 12$
Then	$4 \times 7 =$ _____	$6 \times 7 =$ _____	$8 \times 7 =$ _____	$4 \times 6 =$ _____

b)

If	$3 \times 6 = 18$	$4 \times 6 = 24$	$2 \times 8 = 16$	$4 \times 8 = 32$
Then	$6 \times 6 =$ _____	$8 \times 6 =$ _____	$4 \times 8 =$ _____	$8 \times 8 =$ _____

c)

If	$2 \times 9 = 18$	$3 \times 9 = 27$	$4 \times 9 = 36$	$2 \times 12 = 24$
Then	$4 \times 9 =$ _____	_____ $\times 9 =$ _____	_____ $\times 9 =$ _____	_____ $\times 12 =$ _____

6. Double 2 times the number to find 4 times the number. Then find 8 times the number.

a) $2 \times 7 =$ _____

so $4 \times 7 =$ _____

and $8 \times 7 =$ _____

b) $2 \times 8 =$ _____

so $4 \times 8 =$ _____

and $8 \times 8 =$ _____

c) $2 \times 6 =$ _____

so $4 \times 6 =$ _____

and $8 \times 6 =$ _____

7. Calculate the total cost of 2 items.

a) 2 oranges for 42 cents each _____

b) 2 stickers for 37 cents each _____

c) 2 stamps for 48 cents each _____

d) 2 goldfish for 35 cents each _____

BONUS ▶ Use doubles to find 12×4.

$3 \times 4 =$ _____

so $6 \times 4 =$ _____

so $12 \times 4 =$ _____

8. A table is 32 inches long. How long are two tables?

COPYRIGHT © JUMP MATH: NOT TO BE COPIED. US EDITION

23. Multiplication Tables (1)

1. Count the number of squares in the rectangle. Write your answer in the bottom right square. Then write the multiplication sentence.

   a)

   $2 \times 3 = 6$

   b)

   _____

   c)

   _____

   d)

   _____

2. Draw a rectangle for the product of the two numbers. Count the number of squares in the rectangle. Write the answer in the bottom right square of the rectangle.

   a) 2×3

×	1	2	3	4	5
1					
2			6		
3					
4					
5					

   b) 3×4

×	1	2	3	4	5
1					
2					
3					
4					
5					

   c) 4×2

×	1	2	3	4	5
1					
2					
3					
4					
5					

   d) 2×5

×	1	2	3	4	5
1					
2					
3					
4					
5					

COPYRIGHT © JUMP MATH: NOT TO BE COPIED. US EDITION

Tony wants to use the table to find 3×4.

He draws a rectangle starting at the dot. The rectangle has 3 rows of 4 squares.

The answer is the number in the bottom right corner of the rectangle.

So $3 \times 4 = 12$

×	1	2	3	4	5
1	1	2	3	4	5
2	2	4	6	8	10
3	3	6	9	12	15
4	4	8	12	16	20
5	5	10	15	20	25

3. Use Tony's method to multiply.

a) 2×4

×	1	2	3	4	5
1	1	2	3	4	5
2	2	4	6	8	10
3	3	6	9	12	15
4	4	8	12	16	20
5	5	10	15	20	25

So $2 \times 4 =$ _____

b) 5×3

×	1	2	3	4	5
1	1	2	3	4	5
2	2	4	6	8	10
3	3	6	9	12	15
4	4	8	12	16	20
5	5	10	15	20	25

So $5 \times 3 =$ _____

c) 4×2

×	1	2	3	4	5
1	1	2	3	4	5
2	2	4	6	8	10
3	3	6	9	12	15
4	4	8	12	16	20
5	5	10	15	20	25

So $4 \times 2 =$ _____

d) 5×4

×	1	2	3	4	5
1	1	2	3	4	5
2	2	4	6	8	10
3	3	6	9	12	15
4	4	8	12	16	20
5	5	10	15	20	25

So $5 \times 4 =$ _____

4. Which two answers from Question 3 are the same? Why is that the case?

COPYRIGHT © JUMP MATH: NOT TO BE COPIED. US EDITION

24. Multiplication Tables (2)

A **multiplication table** shows the product of two numbers.

×	I	2	3	4	⑤	← 2nd number
I	I	2	3	4	5	
②	2	4	6	8	⑩	← product: 2 × 5 = 10

1st number ⟶

1. Use the multiplication table to multiply.

   a) 2 × 7 = _____   b) 3 × 6 = _____

   c) 4 × 8 = _____   d) 5 × 7 = _____

   e) 4 × 6 = _____   f) 3 × 8 = _____

   g) 4 × 7 = _____   h) 4 × 4 = _____

×	I	2	3	4	5	6	7	8
I	I	2	3	4	5	6	7	8
2	2	4	6	8	10	12	14	16
3	3	6	9	12	15	18	21	24
4	4	8	12	16	20	24	28	32
5	5	10	15	20	25	30	35	40

2. Find the missing number.

   a) 3 × 7 = _____   b) 4 × 6 = _____   c) 2 × 8 = _____   d) 5 × 6 = _____

   e) _____ × 4 = 8   f) _____ × 8 = 24   g) _____ × 4 = 12   h) 6 × _____ = 18

   i) _____ × 2 = 14   j) 3 × _____ = 15   k) 4 × 4 = _____   l) _____ × 6 = 36

3. a) Finish the multiplication table.

   b) Describe the pattern in the third row of the table.

   _____

   _____

   c) Fill in the blanks.

   The _____ row is the same as the 2nd column.

   The _____ row is the same as the 3rd column.

   The _____ row is the same as the 4th column.

×	I	2	3	4	5
I	I		3		
2		4		8	
3					
4			12		
5	5				25

COPYRIGHT © JUMP MATH: NOT TO BE COPIED. US EDITION

4. a) Use the completed half to quickly finish the empty half.

×	1	2	3	4	5	6	7	8	9	10
1	1	2	3	4	5	6	7	8	9	10
2		4	6	8	10	12	14	16	18	20
3			9	12	15	18	21	24	27	30
4				16	20	24	28	32	36	40
5					25	30	35	40	45	50
6						36	42	48	54	60
7							49	56	63	70
8								64	72	80
9									81	90
10										100

b) Describe any patterns you see in the row for 8.

_____

_____

c) Look for even and odd numbers in the column for 7. What do you notice?

_____

_____

5. Compare the row for 2 with the row for 4. What do you notice?

2	4	6	8	10	12	14	16	18	20

4	8	12	16	20	24	28	32	36	40

COPYRIGHT © JUMP MATH: NOT TO BE COPIED. US EDITION

25. Sharing When You Know the Number of Sets

Four friends want to share 12 cookies. They set out 4 plates.

They put 1 cookie on each plate, then repeat.

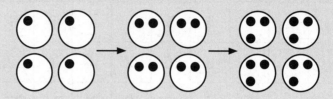

Each plate holds a **set** (or group) of 3 cookies.

When 12 cookies are **divided** (or shared equally) into 4 sets, there are 3 cookies **in each set**.

1. Put an equal number of cookies on each plate.
   Hint: Draw the plates, then place 1 cookie at a time.

   a) 6 cookies   3 plates

   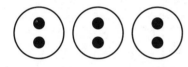

   b) 9 cookies   3 plates

   c) 8 cookies   2 plates

   d) 5 plates   10 cookies

   e) 2 plates   8 cookies

   f) 4 plates   12 cookies

   g) 4 plates   8 cookies

   h) 2 plates   12 cookies

COPYRIGHT © 2014 JUMP MATH: NOT TO BE COPIED. CC EDITION
COPYRIGHT © JUMP MATH: NOT TO BE COPIED. US EDITION

2. Draw dots for the things being shared equally. Draw circles for the sets.

a) 3 wagons

   9 kids

   How many kids in each wagon?

b) 15 stamps

   3 pages

   How many stamps on each page?

_____ kids in each wagon

_____ stamps on each page

c) 4 boats

   12 kids

   How many kids on each boat?

d) 2 boxes

   10 pens

   How many pens in each box?

_____ kids on each boat

_____ pens in each box

3. Draw a picture or make a model to solve the problem.

a) 4 friends share 8 tickets.
   How many tickets does each friend get?

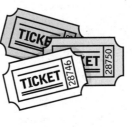

b) 12 chairs are placed in 3 rows.
   How many chairs are in each row?

c) 24 flowers are planted in 6 rows.
   How many flowers are in each row?

d) Roger earned 20 dollars for his work. He worked 5 hours.
   How much did he earn each hour?
   Hint: Draw dots for dollars and circles for hours.

e) Kate earned 15 dollars for her work. She worked 3 hours.
   How much did she earn each hour?

COPYRIGHT © JUMP MATH: NOT TO BE COPIED. US EDITION
COPYRIGHT © 2014 JUMP MATH: NOT TO BE COPIED. CC EDITION

26. Sharing When You Know the Number in Each Set

Ivan has 20 apples. He wants to put 5 apples in each bag.

To find out how many bags he needs, he starts by counting out 5 apples.

He then keeps counting out **sets** of 5 apples until he has used all 20 apples.

He can make 4 bags. When 20 apples are divided into sets of 5 apples, there are 4 sets.

1. Put the correct number of dots in each set.

   a)

   2 dots in each set

   b) ● ● ● ● ● ●

   3 dots in each set

   c)

   2 dots in each set

   d) ● ● ● ● ● ● ● ● ●

   3 dots in each set

   e)

   5 dots in each set

   f) ● ● ● ● ● ● ● ● ● ● ● ●

   3 dots in each set

2. Divide the array into the given number of sets.

   a) sets of 2

   b) sets of 3

   c) groups of 3

   d) groups of 4

3. Draw a picture to solve the problem. Hint: Start by drawing a circle and placing the correct number of dots in the circle.

   a) 12 dots

   4 dots in each set

   How many sets? _____

   b) 15 dots

   5 dots in each set

   How many sets? _____

COPYRIGHT © JUMP MATH: NOT TO BE COPIED. US EDITION

4. Draw dots for the things being divided equally.
Draw circles for the sets.

a) 10 kids

   5 kids in each wagon

   How many wagons?

b) 12 stamps

   4 stamps on each page

   How many pages?

_____ wagons

_____ pages

c) 20 books

   4 books on each shelf

   How many shelves?

d) 15 fish

   5 fish in each tank

   How many tanks?

_____ shelves

_____ tanks

5. Sam has 10 oranges.
He wants to sell bags of 2 oranges.
How many bags can he sell?

6. Emma has 12 books. She
wants to put 3 books in
each bag. How many bags
does she need?

7. Raj has 15 stamps.
He wants to put 5 stamps on each
page of his stamp book. How many
pages will he need?

8. A sailboat can hold 3 kids.
There are 12 kids.
How many sailboats
are needed?

COPYRIGHT © JUMP MATH: NOT TO BE COPIED. US EDITION

27. Sets

12 kids go canoeing.
A canoe holds 3 kids.
There are 4 canoes.

What has been shared or divided into sets?   *Kids.*

How many sets are there?   *There are 4 sets of kids.*

How many are in each set?   *There are 3 kids in each set.*

1. Fill in the blanks.

   a)

   What has been shared or divided

   into sets? _____

   How many sets? _____

   How many in each set? _____

   b)

   What has been shared or divided

   into sets? _____

   How many sets? _____

   How many in each set? _____

2. Draw a picture to show the situation. Use circles for sets and dots for items.

   a) 3 sets   4 items in each set

   b) 4 sets   5 items in each set

   c) 2 groups   3 items in each group

   d) 2 groups   4 items in each group

COPYRIGHT © JUMP MATH: NOT TO BE COPIED. US EDITION

3. Fill in the table.

		What Has Been Shared or Divided into Sets?	How Many Sets?	How Many in Each Set?
a)	15 kids 3 kids in each boat 5 boats	Kids	5	3
b)	5 friends 20 cookies 4 cookies for each friend			
c)	18 oranges 6 boxes 3 oranges in each box			
d)	4 dogs 20 spots 5 spots on each dog			
e)	5 stamps on each page 35 stamps 7 pages			
f)	3 playgrounds 12 swings 4 swings in each playground			
g)	5 people in each house 10 people 2 houses			
h)	20 chairs 5 rows 4 chairs in each row			

COPYRIGHT © JUMP MATH: NOT TO BE COPIED. US EDITION

28. Two Ways of Sharing

Sara has 12 cookies. There are two ways she can share or divide her cookies equally.

Method I:
She can decide how many sets.

Example: She wants to make 3 sets. She draws 3 circles.

She puts one cookie in each circle.

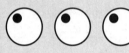

She continues until she uses all 12 cookies.

There are 4 cookies in each set.

Method 2:
She can decide how many in each set.

Example: She puts 4 in each set.

She counts out sets of 4 until she uses all 12 cookies.

   4   8   12

She makes 3 sets.

1. Share 12 dots equally. How many dots are in each set? Place one dot at a time.

   a) 3 sets

   There are _____ dots in each set.

   b) 4 sets

   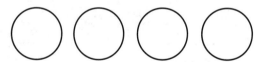

   There are _____ dots in each set.

2. Share 15 dots equally. How many dots are in each set?

   a) 3 sets

   There are _____ dots in each set.

   b) 5 sets

   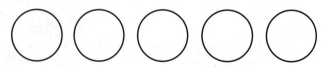

   There are _____ dots in each set.

COPYRIGHT © JUMP MATH: NOT TO BE COPIED. US EDITION

3. Share the triangles equally among the sets.
   Hint: Count the triangles first.

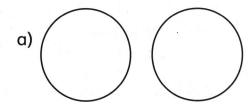

a)

b)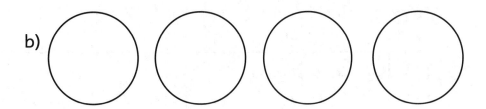

4. Share the squares equally among the sets.

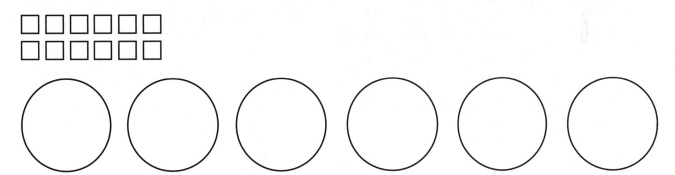

5. Draw a picture to group 12 dots equally.

   a) 3 dots in each set   b) 6 dots in each set

6. Show two ways you could put 10 apples in baskets.

   a) Put 5 apples in each basket.   b) Put 2 apples in each basket.

COPYRIGHT © JUMP MATH: NOT TO BE COPIED. US EDITION

29. Two Ways of Sharing: Word Problems

I. Fill in what you know. Write a question mark for what you don't know.

		What Has Been Shared or Divided into Sets?	How Many Sets?	How Many in Each Set?
a)	Jay has 15 stamps. He puts 5 stamps on each page of his book.	15 stamps	?	5
b)	20 kids go canoeing in 10 canoes.	20 kids	10	?
c)	Don has 15 pens. He puts them into 3 boxes.			
d)	4 friends share 20 apples.			
e)	Grace has 10 cookies. She puts 5 on each plate.			
f)	12 kids go sailing. There are 4 kids in each boat.			
g)	12 fruit bars are shared among 3 kids.			
h)	8 chairs are in 2 rows.			
i)	There are 10 friends. 2 friends fit in a go-cart.			
j)	There are 20 books on a book shelf. Each shelf holds 5 books.			

COPYRIGHT © JUMP MATH: NOT TO BE COPIED. US EDITION

2. Draw dots to show the answer.

a) 10 dots   5 sets

_____ dots in each set

b) 6 dots   3 dots in each set

_____ sets

c) 15 dots   5 dots in each set

_____ sets

d) 8 dots   4 sets

_____ dots in each set

e) 6 chairs in 2 rows

How many chairs are in

each row? _____

f) Ron has 8 pencils.
He puts 2 pencils in each box.

How many boxes does

he use? _____

g) 4 boys share 12 marbles.

How many marbles does each

boy get? _____

h) Pamela has 9 pears.
She gives 3 pears to each friend.

How many friends receive

pears? _____

i) 15 children go sailing in 3 boats.

How many children are in

each boat? _____

j) Peter has 16 stickers.
He puts 4 on a page.

How many pages does

he use? _____

COPYRIGHT © JUMP MATH: NOT TO BE COPIED. US EDITION

30. Division and Addition

You can rewrite any division sentence as an addition sentence.

Example: $12 \div 3 = 4$ because 12 divided into sets of size 3 equals 4 sets.

So   3   +   3   +   3   +   3   =   12.

Adding four 3s equals 12.

1. Draw a picture and write an **addition** sentence for the **division** sentence.

   a) $6 \div 2 = 3$

   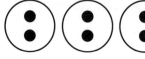

   $\underline{\quad 2 + 2 + 2 = 6 \quad}$

   b) $8 \div 4 = 2$

   $\underline{\qquad\qquad\qquad\qquad}$

   c) $15 \div 5 = 3$

   d) $9 \div 3 = 3$

   $\underline{\qquad\qquad\qquad\qquad}$ $\underline{\qquad\qquad\qquad\qquad}$

2. Draw a picture and write a **division** sentence for the **addition** sentence.

   a) $4 + 4 + 4 = 12$

   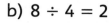

   $\underline{\quad 12 \div 4 = 3 \quad}$

   b) $3 + 3 + 3 + 3 + 3 = 15$

   $\underline{\qquad\qquad\qquad\qquad}$

   c) $6 + 6 + 6 = 18$

   d) $2 + 2 + 2 + 2 + 2 = 10$

   $\underline{\qquad\qquad\qquad\qquad}$ $\underline{\qquad\qquad\qquad\qquad}$

COPYRIGHT © JUMP MATH: NOT TO BE COPIED. US EDITION

31. Dividing by Skip Counting

You can divide by skip counting on a number line. Example: Find 12 ÷ 3.

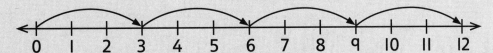

It takes 4 skips of size 3 to get to 12. **3 + 3 + 3 + 3 = 12** so **12 ÷ 3 = 4**

1. Use the number line to complete the division sentence.

a)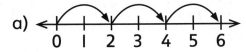

$6 \div 2 = \underline{\quad 3 \quad}$

b)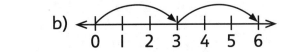

$6 \div 3 = \underline{\quad\quad}$

2. Use the number line to divide.

a)

$8 \div 4 = \underline{\quad\quad}$

b)

$4 \div 4 = \underline{\quad\quad}$

c)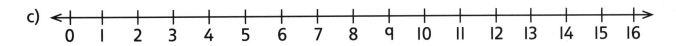

$16 \div 4 = \underline{\quad\quad}$

3. What division sentence does the picture show?

a)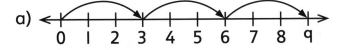

_____

b)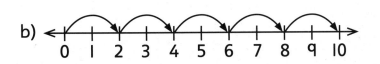

_____

c)

_____

COPYRIGHT © JUMP MATH: NOT TO BE COPIED. US EDITION

You can also divide by skip counting on your fingers.

Example: To find **6 ÷ 2**, count by 2s until you reach 6.

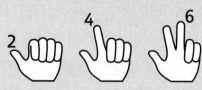

The number of fingers you have up when you stop is the answer.
So 6 ÷ 2 = 3.

4. Find the answer by skip counting on your fingers.

a) 10 ÷ 2 = _____   b) 8 ÷ 2 = _____   c) 4 ÷ 2 = _____   d) 9 ÷ 3 = _____

e) 10 ÷ 5 = _____   f) 15 ÷ 5 = _____   g) 25 ÷ 5 = _____   h) 20 ÷ 5 = _____

i) 12 ÷ 3 = _____   j) 6 ÷ 3 = _____   k) 12 ÷ 2 = _____   l) 5 ÷ 5 = _____

m) 2 ÷ 2 = _____   n) 30 ÷ 5 = _____   o) 15 ÷ 3 = _____   p) 20 ÷ 4 = _____

q) 16 ÷ 2 = _____   r) 3 ÷ 3 = _____   s) 20 ÷ 2 = _____   t) 12 ÷ 4 = _____

5. Fill in the missing numbers on the hands. Then divide by skip counting.

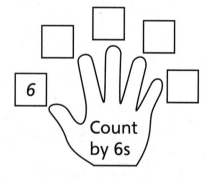

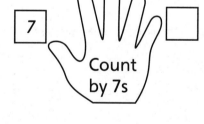

a) 18 ÷ 6 = _____   b) 24 ÷ 6 = _____   c) 12 ÷ 6 = _____

d) 21 ÷ 7 = _____   e) 35 ÷ 7 = _____   f) 28 ÷ 7 = _____

g) 30 ÷ 6 = _____   h) 6 ÷ 6 = _____   i) 7 ÷ 7 = _____

6. Find the answer by skip counting.

a) Three friends share 12 stickers.
   How many stickers does each get?

b) Twenty-four kids sit at 6 tables.
   How many kids are at each table?

COPYRIGHT © JUMP MATH: NOT TO BE COPIED. US EDITION

32. The Two Meanings of Division

David buys 12 fish from a pet store. He has 4 fish bowls.

How many fish can David put in each bowl? David counts by 4s to find out:

4 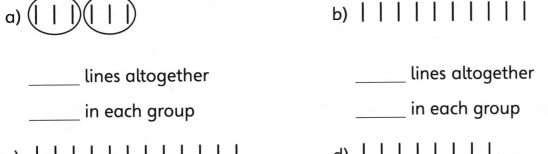 "I could put one fish in each bowl."
(4 are placed)

8
4 "I could put one more in each bowl."
(8 are placed)

8 12
4 "I could put one more in each bowl."
(12 are placed)

He raised 3 fingers, so he knows that **12 ÷ 4 = 3**. He puts 3 fish in each bowl.

1. Count the lines. Then divide the lines into 2 equal groups.
    Hint: Skip count by 2s to decide how many to put in each group.

    a) (| | |) (| | |)

    _____ lines altogether

    _____ in each group

    b) | | | | | | | | | |

    _____ lines altogether

    _____ in each group

    c) | | | | | | | | | | | |

    _____ lines altogether

    _____ in each group

    d) | | | | | | | |

    _____ lines altogether

    _____ in each group

2. Count the objects. Then divide the objects into equal groups.
    Hint: Skip count by the number of groups to decide how many to put in each group.

    a) 3 equal groups

    (| | | |) (| | | |) (| | | |)

    b) 5 equal groups

    ☆ ☆ ☆ ☆ ☆ ☆ ☆ ☆ ☆ ☆

    c) 2 equal groups

    d) 4 equal groups

COPYRIGHT © JUMP MATH: NOT TO BE COPIED. US EDITION

Here are two ways to describe the picture below.

When 15 things are divided into 5 sets, there are 3 things in each set: 15 ÷ 5 = 3.

When 15 things are divided into sets of size 3, there are 5 sets: 15 ÷ 3 = 5.

3. Fill in the blanks. Then write two division sentences.

a) ||||| |||||

_____ lines _____ sets

_____ lines in each set

_____ ÷ _____ = _____

_____ ÷ _____ = _____

b) ||| ||| |||

_____ lines _____ sets

_____ lines in each set

_____ ÷ _____ = _____

_____ ÷ _____ = _____

c) || || || || ||

_____ lines _____ sets

_____ lines in each set

_____ ÷ _____ = _____

_____ ÷ _____ = _____

4. Fill in the blanks. Then write two division sentences.

a)

_____ squares _____ sets

_____ squares in each set

_____

_____

b)

_____ dots _____ sets

_____ dots in each set

_____

_____

c)

_____ stars _____ sets

_____ stars in each set

_____

_____

5. Solve the problem by drawing a picture. Then write a division sentence for your answer.

a) 9 triangles, 3 sets
How many triangles in each set?

b) 12 squares, 4 squares in each set
How many sets?

c) 30 people, 5 vans
How many people in each van?

d) 20 children, 4 in each tent
How many tents?

COPYRIGHT © JUMP MATH: NOT TO BE COPIED. US EDITION

33. Division and Multiplication

Remember: 10 ÷ 2 = 5 tells us that 10 ÷ 5 = 2, and 5 × 2 = 10 tells us that
2 × 5 = 10. You can rewrite any **division** sentence as a **multiplication** sentence.

Example: 10 divided into sets of size 2 equals 5 sets or **10 ÷ 2 = 5**.

You can rewrite this as: 5 sets of size 2 equals 10 or **5 × 2 = 10**.

I. Write two multiplication sentences and two division sentences
   for the picture.

a)

_____

_____

_____

_____

b)

_____

_____

_____

_____

c)

_____

_____

_____

d)

_____

_____

_____

COPYRIGHT © JUMP MATH: NOT TO BE COPIED. US EDITION

2. Review the 2, 3, 4, and 5 times tables. Complete the multiplication sentence. Then divide.

a) $\boxed{5} \times 4 = 20$

   $20 \div 4 = \boxed{5}$

b) $2 \times \boxed{} = 12$

   $12 \div 2 = \boxed{}$

c) $5 \times \boxed{} = 20$

   $20 \div 5 = \boxed{}$

d) $4 \times \boxed{} = 28$

   $28 \div 4 = \boxed{}$

e) $5 \times \boxed{} = 45$

   $45 \div 5 = \boxed{}$

f) $3 \times \boxed{} = 21$

   $21 \div 3 = \boxed{}$

g) $\boxed{} \times 3 = 24$

   $24 \div 3 = \boxed{}$

h) $4 \times \boxed{} = 24$

   $24 \div 4 = \boxed{}$

i) $\boxed{} \times 3 = 18$

   $18 \div 3 = \boxed{}$

3. Review the 6, 7, 8, and 9 times tables. Complete the multiplication sentence. Then divide.

a) $9 \times \boxed{} = 18$

   $18 \div 9 = \boxed{}$

b) $8 \times \boxed{} = 40$

   $40 \div 8 = \boxed{}$

c) $7 \times \boxed{} = 21$

   $21 \div 7 = \boxed{}$

d) $8 \times \boxed{} = 32$

   $32 \div 8 = \boxed{}$

e) $6 \times \boxed{} = 42$

   $42 \div 6 = \boxed{}$

f) $\boxed{} \times 7 = 49$

   $49 \div 7 = \boxed{}$

g) $\boxed{} \times 6 = 48$

   $48 \div 6 = \boxed{}$

h) $8 \times \boxed{} = 64$

   $64 \div 8 = \boxed{}$

i) $9 \times \boxed{} = 36$

   $36 \div 9 = \boxed{}$

j) $6 \times \boxed{} = 12$

   $12 \div 6 = \boxed{}$

k) $7 \times \boxed{} = 28$

   $28 \div 7 = \boxed{}$

l) $\boxed{} \times 9 = 54$

   $54 \div 9 = \boxed{}$

m) $\boxed{} \times 7 = 56$

   $56 \div 7 = \boxed{}$

n) $5 \times \boxed{} = 35$

   $35 \div 5 = \boxed{}$

o) $6 \times \boxed{} = 36$

   $36 \div 6 = \boxed{}$

COPYRIGHT © JUMP MATH: NOT TO BE COPIED. US EDITION

4. Fill in the blanks.

a) [|| | || | ||]

_____ lines in total

_____ lines in each set

_____ sets

b) [|||| | |||| | |||| | ||||]

_____ lines in total

_____ sets

_____ lines in each set

c) [|||| | |||| | ||||]

_____ lines in each group

_____ groups

_____ lines

d) [|| | || | || | || | || | ||]

_____ lines in each group

_____ lines

_____ groups

5. Draw a picture to show the situation.

a) 12 lines altogether, 3 lines in each set, 4 sets

b) 8 lines, 4 lines in each set, 2 sets

c) 5 sets, 3 lines in each set, 15 lines in total

d) 12 lines, 2 sets, 6 lines in each set

e) 10 lines, 5 in each set, 2 sets

6. Draw a picture to show the situation. Then write two division sentences and two multiplication sentences.

a) 20 lines, 5 sets, 4 lines in each set

b) 15 lines, 5 lines in each set, 3 sets

7. Draw a picture to find the missing information.

a) 5 lines in each set

_____ sets

15 lines altogether

b) 18 lines

_____ lines in each set

3 sets

c) _____ lines in total

3 groups

4 lines in each group

COPYRIGHT © JUMP MATH: NOT TO BE COPIED. US EDITION

34. Knowing When to Multiply or Divide

1. Multiply or divide to find the missing information (?).

	Total Number of Things	Number of Sets	Number in Each Set	Multiplication or Division Sentence
a)	?	8	2	$8 \times 2 = 16$
b)	27	3	?	$27 \div 3 = 9$
c)	20	?	5	
d)	10	2	?	
e)	?	4	8	
f)	21	7	?	
g)	32	8	?	
h)	45	?	9	
i)	64	8	?	
j)	81	9	?	
k)	72	?	8	
l)	16	4	?	
m)	28	?	7	
n)	42	6	?	
o)	?	8	9	

COPYRIGHT © JUMP MATH: NOT TO BE COPIED. US EDITION

2. Write a multiplication or division sentence to solve the problem.

a) 15 things in total
5 things in each set

_____

How many sets?

_____

b) 5 sets
4 things in each set

_____

How many in total?

_____

c) 24 things in total
6 sets

_____

How many in each set?

_____

d) 21 groups
7 things in each group

_____

How many in total?

_____

e) 2 things in each set
12 things in total

_____

How many sets?

_____

f) 5 groups
45 things in total

_____

How many in
each group? _____

g) 5 things in each set
4 sets

_____

How many in total?

_____

h) 8 things in each set
3 sets

_____

How many in total?

_____

i) 16 things in total
8 sets

_____

How many in each set?

_____

j) 3 things in each set
6 sets

_____

How many in total?

_____

k) 12 things in total
4 sets

_____

How many in each set?

_____

l) 20 things in total
4 sets

_____

How many in each set?

_____

3. Make up your own problem with things in sets.
Draw a picture to solve it.

COPYRIGHT © JUMP MATH: NOT TO BE COPIED. US EDITION

35. Knowing When to Multiply or Divide: Word Problems

1. Fill in the table. Use a question mark to show what you don't know.

		Total number of things	Number of sets	Number in each set	Multiplication or division sentence
a)	20 people 4 vans	20	4	?	$20 \div 4 = ?$
b)	3 marbles in each jar 6 jars	?	6	3	$6 \times 3 = ?$
c)	15 flowers 5 pots				
d)	4 chairs at each table 2 tables				
e)	20 flowers 4 in each row				
f)	6 seats in each row 2 rows				
g)	18 houses 9 houses on each block				
h)	15 chairs 3 rows				
i)	6 tents 3 kids in each tent				
j)	9 boxes 3 sea shells in each box				
k)	6 legs on each insect 42 legs				

2. Find the missing number in each part of Question 1.

COPYRIGHT © JUMP MATH: NOT TO BE COPIED. US EDITION

The fact family for the multiplication sentence **3 × 5 = 15** is:

$$3 \times 5 = 15 \qquad 5 \times 3 = 15 \qquad 15 \div 3 = 5 \qquad 15 \div 5 = 3$$

3. Complete the fact family for the given multiplication or division sentence.

a) $4 \times 2 = 8$

b) $5 \times 6 = 30$

c) $10 \div 2 = 5$

_____

_____

_____

_____

_____

_____

_____

_____

_____

d) $12 \div 4 = 3$

e) $9 \times 3 = 27$

f) $6 \times 8 = 48$

_____

_____

_____

_____

_____

_____

_____

_____

_____

4. Anwar plants 24 trees in 3 rows. How many trees are in each row?

5. Alex plants 4 rows of trees with 7 in each row. How many trees did he plant?

6. A canoe can hold 3 people.

a) How many canoes are needed for 21 people?

b) How many people can go canoeing with 5 canoes?

7. Tickets for the museum cost $6.

a) How many tickets can Mandy buy with $18?

b) How much will 5 tickets cost?

BONUS ▶ Kim has $13. If she buys 2 tickets, how much money will she have left?

COPYRIGHT © JUMP MATH: NOT TO BE COPIED. US EDITION

36. Multiplication and Division (Review)

1. What is the fact family for $2 \times 3 = 6$?

2. Find the mystery number.

a) I am a multiple of 2.
   I am greater than 10 and less than 13.

b) I am a multiple of 3.
   I am between 13 and 20.
   I am an even number.

3. A hummingbird feeds 6 times each hour.
How many times does it feed in 7 hours?

4. Apple trees in an orchard are planted in 7 rows.
There are 4 trees in each row.

a) How many trees are in the orchard?

b) How did you find your answer? Mental math?
   Skip counting? A picture?

5. 6 is twice as much as (or double) 3. Is 6×5 twice as much
as 3×5? Use an array to decide.

6. Fill in the blanks. Then write two division sentences and
one multiplication sentence using the boxes.

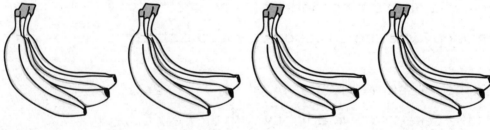

_____ bananas

_____ bananas in each bunch

_____ bunches

$$\boxed{} \div \boxed{} = \boxed{} \qquad \boxed{} \div \boxed{} = \boxed{} \qquad \boxed{} \times \boxed{} = \boxed{}$$

COPYRIGHT © JUMP MATH: NOT TO BE COPIED. US EDITION

7. A hawk's nest holds at least 3 eggs and at most 5 eggs.

   a) What is the **least** number of eggs 3 nests would hold?

   b) What is the **greatest** number of eggs 3 nests would hold?

8. A shelf is 40 cm long. How many stuffed animals of each type would fit end to end?

a)    b)    c)

       5 cm wide   4 cm wide   8 cm wide

9. Picture A shows that 5 sets of 4 equals 3 sets of 4 plus 2 sets of 4.

A.

What does picture B show?

B.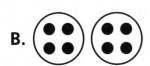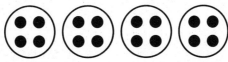

10. Fill in the blanks with the numbers 2, 3, and 4 to make the number sentence true.

   a) _____ × _____ + _____ = 11   b) _____ ÷ _____ + _____ = 5

11. Clara divided one number by another and got the answer 3. What might the numbers have been?

12. Make up a story problem for the number sentence.

   a) 5 × 4 = 20   b) 12 ÷ 3 = 4

COPYRIGHT © JUMP MATH: NOT TO BE COPIED. US EDITION

37. Unit Fractions

There are 4 equal parts.

Each part is one fourth.

One fourth is a fraction.

one fourth or $\frac{1}{4}$ ← number of parts shaded

← number of parts in the whole

You can write fractions with words or numbers.

I. Write the fraction for the equal parts with words and with numbers.

a)

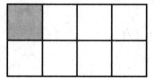

___8___ equal parts

Each part is

__one__ __eighth__ or $\boxed{\dfrac{1}{8}}$.

b)

_____ equal parts

Each part is

_____ _____ or $\boxed{}$.

c)

_____ equal parts

Each part is

_____ _____ or $\boxed{}$.

d)

_____ equal parts

Each part is

_____ _____ or $\boxed{}$.

e)

_____ equal parts

Each part is

_____ _____ or $\boxed{}$.

f)

_____ equal parts

Each part is

_____ _____ or $\boxed{}$.

COPYRIGHT © JUMP MATH: NOT TO BE COPIED. US EDITION

A **unit fraction** has only 1 equal part shaded. $\frac{1}{4}$

2. Write the unit fraction shown by the shaded part of the picture.

a) $\frac{1}{4}$

b)

c)

d)

e)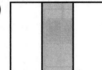

f)

3. Shade the unit fraction.

a) $\frac{1}{5}$

b) $\frac{1}{2}$

c) $\frac{1}{4}$

d) $\frac{1}{10}$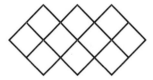

e) $\frac{1}{3}$

f) $\frac{1}{6}$

4. Circle the unit fractions.

$\frac{2}{3}$ $\left(\frac{1}{4}\right)$ $\frac{1}{8}$ $\frac{4}{7}$ $\frac{1}{5}$ $\frac{9}{10}$ $\frac{1}{6}$ $\frac{2}{9}$

5. Circle the pictures that do not show one fourth.

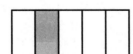

BONUS ▶ Imagine folding a piece of paper to show one fourth.
Draw lines to show the folds. Shade one fourth.

COPYRIGHT © JUMP MATH: NOT TO BE COPIED. US EDITION

38. Writing Fractions

There are 4 equal parts.
3 parts are shaded.

You can write the fraction as $\frac{3}{4}$.

$\frac{3}{4}$ ← The **numerator** tells you 3 parts are shaded.

← The **denominator** tells you 4 parts are in the whole.

I. Count the number of shaded parts and the number of equal parts in the picture. Then write the fraction shown by the shaded parts.

a)

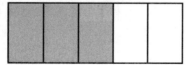

__3__ shaded parts

__5__ equal parts

The fraction is $\boxed{\frac{3}{5}}$.

b)

_____ shaded parts

_____ equal parts

The fraction is $\boxed{}$.

c)

_____ shaded parts

_____ equal parts

The fraction is $\boxed{}$.

d)

_____ shaded parts

_____ equal parts

The fraction is $\boxed{}$.

2. Write the fraction shown by the shaded part or parts.

a)

 $\boxed{\frac{2}{5}}$

b)

 $\boxed{}$

c)

 $\boxed{}$

d)

 $\boxed{}$

e)

 $\boxed{}$

f)

 $\boxed{}$

COPYRIGHT © JUMP MATH: NOT TO BE COPIED. US EDITION

3. Shade parts to show the fraction.

a) $\frac{3}{4}$

b) $\frac{2}{3}$

c) $\frac{1}{5}$

d) $\frac{7}{8}$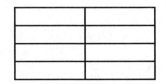

e) $\frac{5}{6}$

f) $\frac{2}{2}$

4. Write a fraction for the parts that are not shaded.

a) 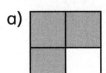 $\boxed{\frac{1}{4}}$

b)

c)

d)

e)

f)

5. Circle the pictures that do not show $\frac{2}{3}$.

 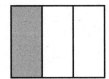

6. For each picture that you circled in Question 5, explain why it does not show $\frac{2}{3}$.

7. You have $\frac{2}{5}$ of a pie.

a) What does the denominator of the fraction tell you?

b) What does the numerator of the fraction tell you?

BONUS ▶ If $\frac{5}{8}$ of a circle is shaded, what fraction of the circle is not shaded?

Hint: Draw a picture.

COPYRIGHT © JUMP MATH: NOT TO BE COPIED. US EDITION

39. Equal Parts of Shapes

I. Shade one half of the shape in two different ways.

a)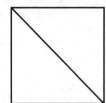

b)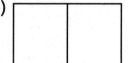

c)

d)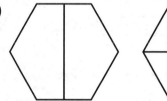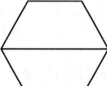

e)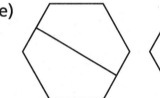

f)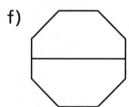

2. Write "yes" or "no" to answer the question for each part in Question I.

a) Are the fractions the same?

b) Do the equal parts look the same?

3. Shade one fourth of the shape in different ways.

a)

b)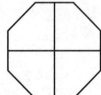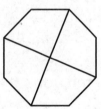

4. Write "yes" or "no" to answer the question for each part in Question 3.

a) Are the fractions the same?

b) Do the equal parts look the same?

COPYRIGHT © JUMP MATH: NOT TO BE COPIED. US EDITION

5. Add a line to the picture to make 4 equal parts.

a)

b)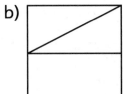

BONUS ▶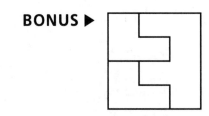

6. Add a line to the picture to make 6 equal parts.

a)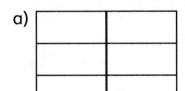

b)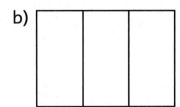

c)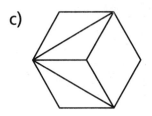

d)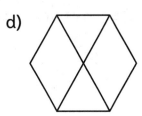

7. John must shade in one fifth of the big square.

Is his answer correct? _____

Explain. _____

_____

_____

_____

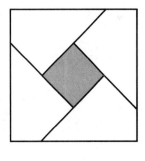

BONUS ▶ Show two different ways to divide a rectangle into 8 equal rectangles.

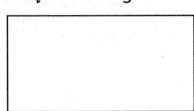

COPYRIGHT © JUMP MATH: NOT TO BE COPIED. US EDITION

40. Different Shapes, Same Fractions

1. Draw a line to create 2 equal parts. Then shade $\frac{1}{2}$ of the whole.

a)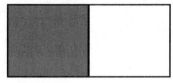

b)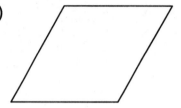

c)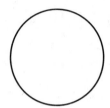

d)

e)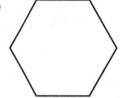

BONUS ▶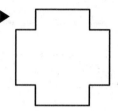

2. Draw a line to create 3 equal parts. Then shade $\frac{2}{3}$ of the whole.

a)

b)

c)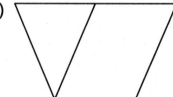

d)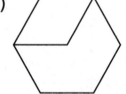

e)

BONUS ▶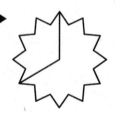

3. Draw a line to create 4 equal parts. Then shade $\frac{3}{4}$ of the whole.

a)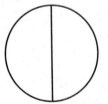

b)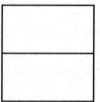

c)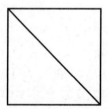

d)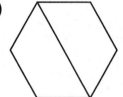

e)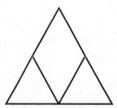

BONUS ▶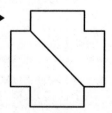

COPYRIGHT © JUMP MATH: NOT TO BE COPIED. US EDITION

4. One half of a shape is shaded. Outline the whole shape.

a)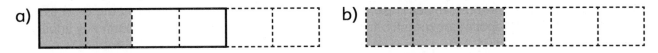

b)

c)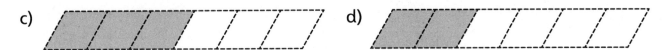

d)

e)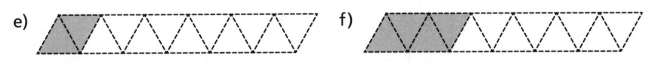

f)

g)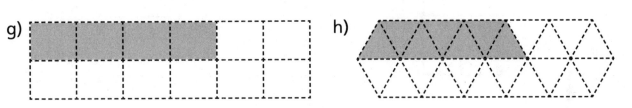

h)

5. One third of a shape is shaded. Outline the whole shape.

a)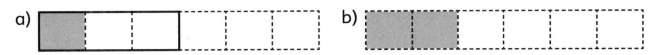

b)

c)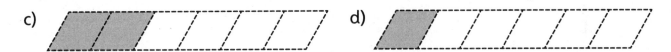

d)

e)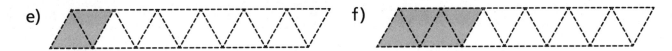

f)

g)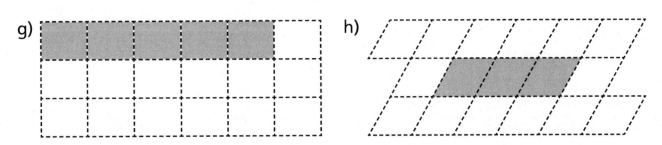

h)

BONUS ▶ One fourth of a shape is shaded. Outline the whole shape.

COPYRIGHT © JUMP MATH: NOT TO BE COPIED. US EDITION

41. Comparing Fractions (Introduction)

1. Shade the fraction of the strip.

a) $\dfrac{3}{4}$

b) $\dfrac{2}{3}$

c) $\dfrac{2}{5}$

d) $\dfrac{7}{8}$

2. Which strip has more shaded? Circle the greater fraction.

a) $\dfrac{2}{5}$
$\boxed{\dfrac{3}{5}}$ (circled)

b) $\dfrac{3}{4}$
$\dfrac{1}{4}$

c) $\dfrac{5}{8}$
$\dfrac{3}{8}$

d) $\dfrac{1}{3}$
$\dfrac{2}{3}$

$\dfrac{7}{8}$ is greater than $\dfrac{3}{8}$ because more of the whole is shaded.

$\dfrac{7}{8}$

$\dfrac{3}{8}$

3. Shade the fractions of the strips. Then circle the greater fraction.

a) $\left(\dfrac{3}{5}\right)$ (circled)
$\dfrac{2}{5}$

b) $\dfrac{3}{4}$
$\dfrac{1}{4}$

c) $\dfrac{5}{8}$
$\dfrac{7}{8}$

d) $\dfrac{3}{6}$
$\dfrac{5}{6}$

COPYRIGHT © JUMP MATH: NOT TO BE COPIED. US EDITION

4. Shade the fractions of the strips. Then circle the smaller fraction.

a) 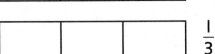 $\frac{2}{3}$

$\frac{1}{3}$

b) 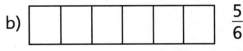 $\frac{5}{6}$

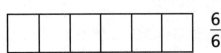 $\frac{6}{6}$

c)  $\frac{3}{7}$

$\frac{6}{7}$

d) 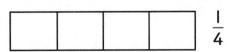 $\frac{0}{4}$

$\frac{1}{4}$

"5 is greater than 3" is written as 5 > 3.   "3 is less than 5" is written as 3 < 5.

5. Circle the greater fraction. Then use the correct sign (> or <) to compare the fractions.

a) 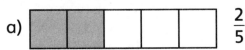 $\frac{2}{5}$

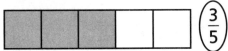 $\left(\frac{3}{5}\right)$

$\frac{2}{5}$ $\boxed{<}$ $\frac{3}{5}$

b) 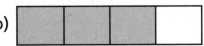 $\frac{3}{4}$

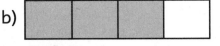 $\frac{1}{4}$

$\frac{3}{4}$ $\square$ $\frac{1}{4}$

c) 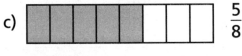 $\frac{5}{8}$

$\frac{3}{8}$

$\frac{5}{8}$ $\square$ $\frac{3}{8}$

d) 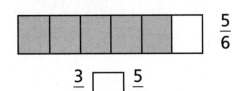 $\frac{3}{6}$

$\frac{5}{6}$

$\frac{3}{6}$ $\square$ $\frac{5}{6}$

6. Nancy looked at the pictures and said that $\frac{1}{3} > \frac{2}{3}$. Explain her mistake.

$\frac{1}{3}$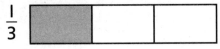

$\frac{2}{3}$

COPYRIGHT © JUMP MATH: NOT TO BE COPIED. US EDITION

42. Equal Parts and Models of Fractions

I. Use the centimeter ruler to divide the line into equal parts.
Mark with ticks on the line.

a) 5 equal parts

b) 4 equal parts

c) 3 equal parts

d) 8 equal parts

2. Use the inch ruler to divide the line into equal parts.

a) 3 equal parts

b) 2 equal parts

3. Use a ruler to join the marks and divide the box into equal parts.

a) 5 equal parts

b) 8 equal parts

4. Use a centimeter ruler to mark the box in centimeters. Then divide
the box into equal parts.

a) 3 equal parts

b) 5 equal parts

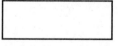

c) 2 equal parts

d) 7 equal parts

COPYRIGHT © JUMP MATH: NOT TO BE COPIED. US EDITION

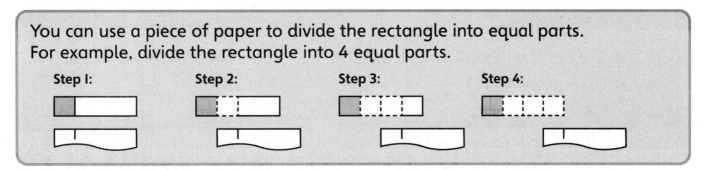

You can use a piece of paper to divide the rectangle into equal parts.
For example, divide the rectangle into 4 equal parts.

Step 1:   **Step 2:**   **Step 3:**   **Step 4:**

5. Use a piece of paper to divide the rectangle into equal parts.

   a) 3 equal parts   b) 5 equal parts

6. Use a ruler or a piece of paper to find what fraction of the rectangle is shaded.

   a) $\dfrac{1}{3}$

   b)

   c)

   d)

7. Use the ruler to draw the rest of the whole shape. Shade the fraction named.

   a) $\dfrac{3}{4}$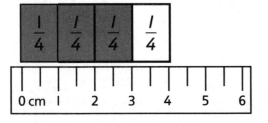

   b) $\dfrac{4}{5}$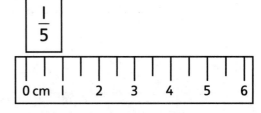

   c) $\dfrac{2}{3}$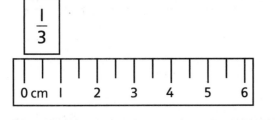

   d) $\dfrac{3}{6}$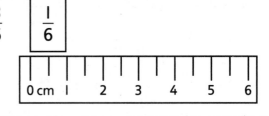

COPYRIGHT © JUMP MATH: NOT TO BE COPIED. US EDITION

43. Fractions on a Number Line

You can also use number lines to show fractions.

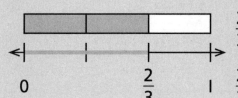

$\frac{2}{3}$ of the strip is shaded.

$\frac{2}{3}$ of the number line from 0 to 1 is shaded.

1. Write what fraction of the strip is shaded. Then label the fraction on the number line.

a) 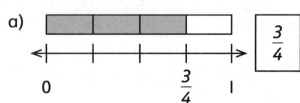 $\boxed{\dfrac{3}{4}}$

b)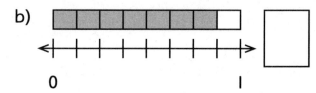

c)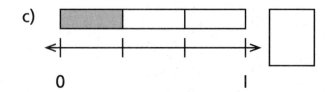

d)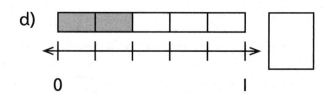

e)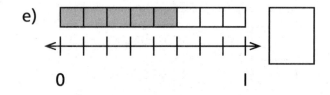

f)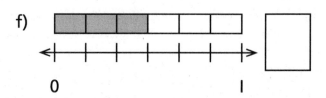

2. Shade the fraction of the strip that shows the fraction on the number line.

a)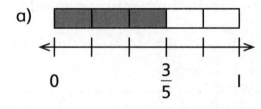

b)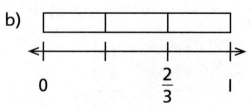

c)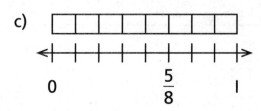

d)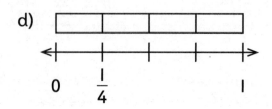

COPYRIGHT © JUMP MATH: NOT TO BE COPIED. US EDITION

You can label a number line with fractions.

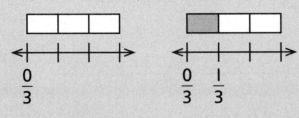 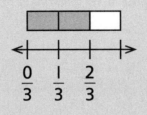 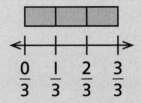

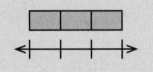

There are 3 equal parts in the whole.

3. Count the number of parts in the whole. Then label all the fractions on the number line.

a)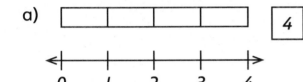

$\boxed{4}$

$\frac{0}{4}$ $\frac{1}{4}$ $\frac{2}{4}$ $\frac{3}{4}$ $\frac{4}{4}$

b) 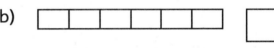 $\square$

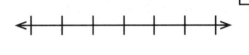

c) 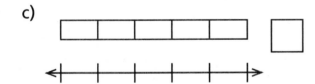 $\square$

d)  $\square$

e) 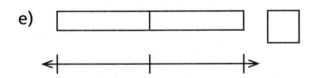 $\square$

f) 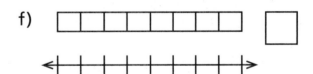 $\square$

BONUS ▶ Each inch on a six-inch ruler needs to be marked with fourths.

How many fourths will be marked on the entire ruler? _____
Mark them.

COPYRIGHT © JUMP MATH: NOT TO BE COPIED. US EDITION

44. Fractions on a Number Line (Advanced)

1. The dot on the number line marks a fraction. Count the equal parts and label the dot.

a)

b)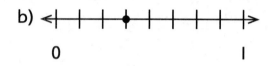

c)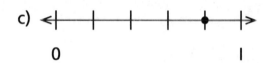

d)

e)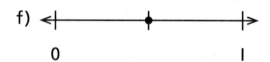

f)

g)

h)

2. Fold paper to mark and label the fractions on the number line.

a) fourths
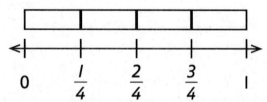

b) halves
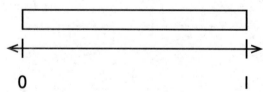

c) thirds
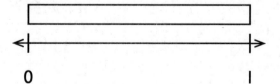

d) eighths
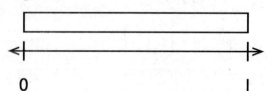

COPYRIGHT © JUMP MATH: NOT TO BE COPIED. US EDITION

3. Divide the number line from 0 to I into equal parts. Then mark the fraction.

a) 3 equal parts and mark $\frac{2}{3}$

0           $\frac{2}{3}$ I

b) 2 equal parts and mark $\frac{1}{2}$

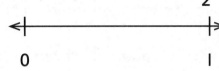

0   I

c) 4 equal parts and mark $\frac{1}{4}$

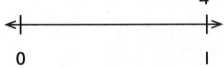

0   I

d) 8 equal parts and mark $\frac{5}{8}$

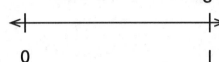

0   I

4. Circle the larger fraction on the number line.

a)

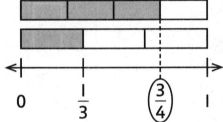

0    $\frac{1}{3}$ $\left(\frac{3}{4}\right)$ I

b)

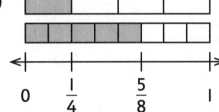

0    $\frac{1}{4}$ $\frac{5}{8}$ I

c)

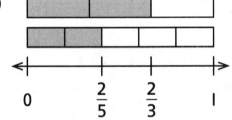

0    $\frac{2}{5}$ $\frac{2}{3}$ I

d)

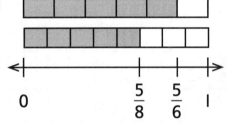

0       $\frac{5}{8}$ $\frac{5}{6}$ I

> You can use number lines to compare fractions. $\frac{3}{4}$ is farther to the right on the number line than $\frac{1}{3}$, so $\frac{3}{4}$ is greater than $\frac{1}{3}$. You write $\frac{3}{4} > \frac{1}{3}$.

5. Several fractions with different denominators have been marked on the number line.

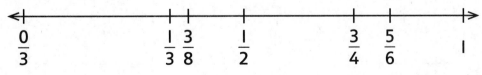

$\frac{0}{3}$ $\frac{1}{3}$ $\frac{3}{8}$ $\frac{1}{2}$ $\frac{3}{4}$ $\frac{5}{6}$ I

Write < (less than) or > (greater than) to compare fractions.

a) $\frac{1}{3}$ ☐ $\frac{1}{2}$ b) $\frac{5}{6}$ ☐ $\frac{3}{8}$ c) $\frac{3}{4}$ ☐ $\frac{3}{8}$ d) $\frac{1}{2}$ ☐ $\frac{5}{6}$

COPYRIGHT © JUMP MATH: NOT TO BE COPIED. US EDITION

45. Equivalent Fractions

Two thirds equals four sixths because the same amount of the whole is shaded.

$\frac{2}{3}$ and $\frac{4}{6}$ are **equivalent fractions**.

$\frac{2}{3}$

$\frac{4}{6}$

I. Write the equivalent fraction.

a) 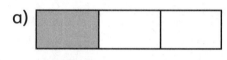 $\frac{1}{3} = \boxed{}$

b) 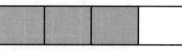 $\frac{3}{4} = \boxed{}$

c) $\frac{2}{5} = \boxed{}$

d) 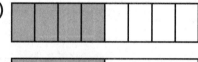 $\frac{4}{8} = \boxed{}$

2. Use dots to mark the equivalent fractions on the number line.

a) 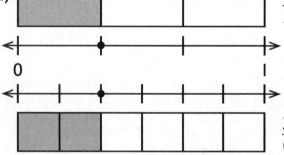 $\frac{1}{3}$

$\frac{2}{6}$

b) 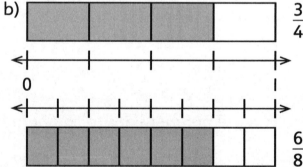 $\frac{3}{4}$

$\frac{6}{8}$

c) $\frac{2}{5}$

$\frac{4}{10}$

d) 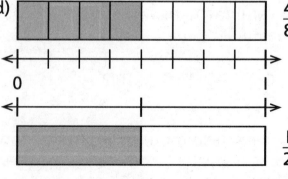 $\frac{4}{8}$

$\frac{1}{2}$

COPYRIGHT © JUMP MATH: NOT TO BE COPIED. US EDITION

Two fractions are equivalent if you mark them on a number line at the same place.

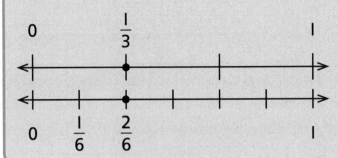

$\dfrac{1}{3}$ and $\dfrac{2}{6}$ are equivalent fractions.

You write $\dfrac{1}{3} = \dfrac{2}{6}$.

3. Use the number lines to find equivalent fractions.

a)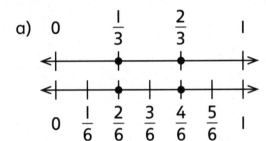

$\dfrac{1}{3} = \boxed{}$ $\dfrac{2}{3} = \boxed{}$

b)

$\dfrac{1}{4} = \boxed{}$ $\dfrac{3}{4} = \boxed{}$

c)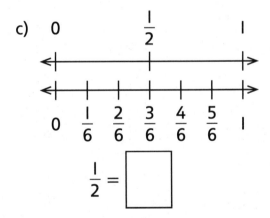

$\dfrac{1}{2} = \boxed{}$

d)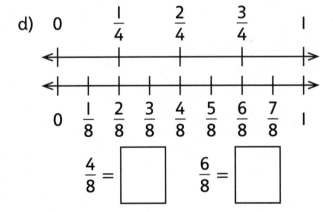

$\dfrac{4}{8} = \boxed{}$ $\dfrac{6}{8} = \boxed{}$

4. Use the number lines to write an equivalent fraction.

a)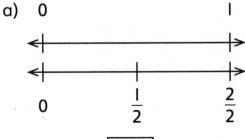

$1 = \boxed{\dfrac{2}{2}}$

b)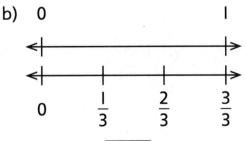

$1 = \boxed{}$

COPYRIGHT © JUMP MATH: NOT TO BE COPIED. US EDITION

5. Use the number lines to write an equivalent fraction.

a)   0   1

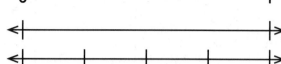

0        $\frac{1}{4}$

| = [ ]

b)   0   1

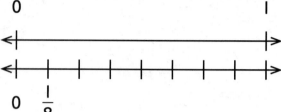

0    $\frac{1}{8}$

| = [ ]

6. Write an equivalent fraction using the given denominator.

a) $| = \dfrac{}{3}$ b) $| = \dfrac{}{6}$ c) $| = \dfrac{}{16}$ **BONUS ▶** $| = \dfrac{}{199}$

Equivalent fractions name equal parts of the same whole.

 $\dfrac{3}{4}$ Cut each part into 2 new parts $\dfrac{6}{8}$ ← parts shaded ← equal parts So $\dfrac{3}{4} = \dfrac{6}{8}$.

---

7. Each part in the whole is cut into 2 equal parts. Write the equivalent fractions.

a)
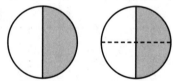

$\boxed{\dfrac{1}{2}} = \boxed{\dfrac{2}{4}}$

b)
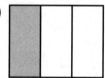 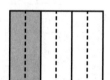

[ ] = [ ]

c)
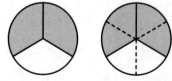

[ ] = [ ]

d)
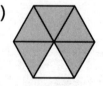

[ ] = [ ]

COPYRIGHT © JUMP MATH: NOT TO BE COPIED. US EDITION

8. Each part in the whole is cut into 3 equal parts. Write the equivalent fractions.

a)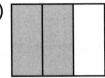

$$\boxed{\dfrac{2}{3}} = \boxed{\dfrac{6}{9}}$$

b)

$$\boxed{} = \boxed{}$$

c)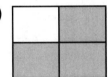

$$\boxed{} = \boxed{}$$

BONUS ▶

$$\boxed{} = \boxed{}$$

9. Draw lines that divide each part in the whole to show the equivalent fraction.

a)

$$\dfrac{2}{5} = \dfrac{4}{10}$$

b)

$$\dfrac{3}{4} = \dfrac{6}{8}$$

c)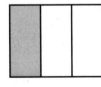

$$\dfrac{1}{3} = \dfrac{3}{9}$$

d)

$$\dfrac{1}{2} = \dfrac{3}{6}$$

 BONUS ▶ Kate cut each part in the whole into more equal parts and was able to show $\dfrac{2}{3} = \dfrac{10}{15}$. Into how many equal parts did she divide each part of the whole?

COPYRIGHT © JUMP MATH: NOT TO BE COPIED. US EDITION

46. Fractions Greater Than 1 on a Number Line

The numbers 0, 1, 2, 3, 4, and so on, are **whole numbers**.

A number line can be labeled with whole numbers or fractions.

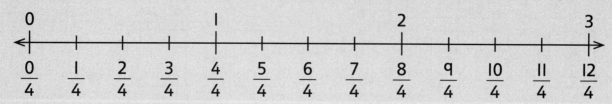

1. Count by the given fraction to label the number line.

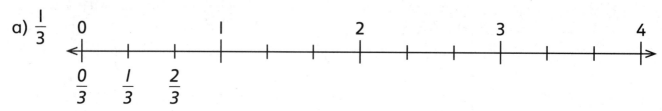

a) $\dfrac{1}{3}$

$\dfrac{0}{3}$ $\dfrac{1}{3}$ $\dfrac{2}{3}$

b) $\dfrac{1}{8}$

$\dfrac{0}{8}$

c) $\dfrac{1}{2}$

$\dfrac{0}{2}$

d) $\dfrac{1}{5}$

$\dfrac{0}{5}$ $\dfrac{1}{5}$ $\dfrac{2}{5}$

2. Use the number lines in Question 1 to find a whole number that is equivalent to the fraction.

a) $\dfrac{6}{3} = \underline{\ 2\ }$

b) $\dfrac{15}{5} = \underline{\hspace{2em}}$

c) $\dfrac{16}{8} = \underline{\hspace{2em}}$

d) $\dfrac{8}{2} = \underline{\hspace{2em}}$

e) $\dfrac{12}{2} = \underline{\hspace{2em}}$

f) $\dfrac{0}{8} = \underline{\hspace{2em}}$

g) $\dfrac{3}{3} = \underline{\hspace{2em}}$

h) $\dfrac{5}{5} = \underline{\hspace{2em}}$

BONUS ▶ What whole number is equivalent to the fraction $\dfrac{999}{999}$? $\underline{\hspace{2em}}$

COPYRIGHT © JUMP MATH: NOT TO BE COPIED. US EDITION

3. Circle the fractions that are equivalent to whole numbers.

a)
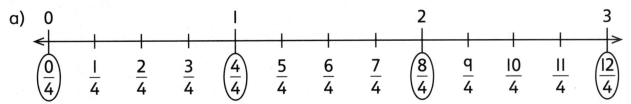

b)
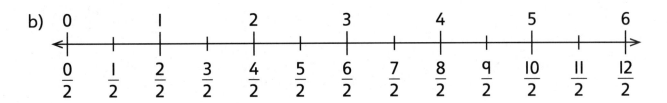

c)
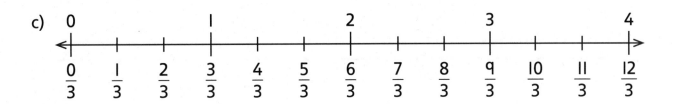

d)
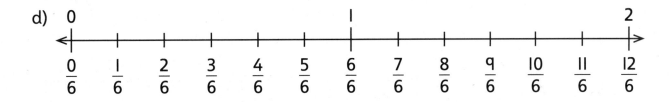

4. Label the whole numbers on the number line.

a) Each mark is one fourth.

b) Each mark is one half.

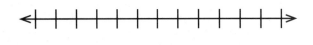

c) Each mark is one third.

d) Each mark is one sixth.

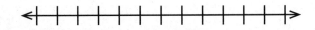
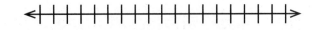

e) Each mark is one eighth.

COPYRIGHT © JUMP MATH: NOT TO BE COPIED. US EDITION

5. Place a dot where the fraction should go on the number line.

a) $\frac{7}{4}$ 0   1   2

b) $\frac{9}{2}$ 0   1   2   3   4   5   6

c) $\frac{8}{3}$ 0   1   2   3

d) $\frac{11}{8}$ 0   1   2

6. Count the parts in each whole. Then write the fraction to label the dot.

a)   0   1   2   3

____4____ parts in each whole   fraction $\boxed{\dfrac{7}{4}}$

b)   0   1   2   3   4

_____ parts in each whole   fraction $\boxed{}$

c)   0   1   2   3   4   5   6

_____ parts in each whole   fraction $\boxed{}$

d)   0   1   2

_____ parts in each whole   fraction $\boxed{}$

COPYRIGHT © JUMP MATH: NOT TO BE COPIED. US EDITION

7. Use the number lines to find equivalent fractions.

a)

$$\frac{2}{3} = \boxed{\frac{4}{6}} \qquad \frac{5}{3} = \boxed{} \qquad \frac{4}{3} = \boxed{} \qquad \frac{2}{6} = \boxed{}$$

b)

$$\frac{3}{2} = \boxed{} \qquad \frac{5}{2} = \boxed{} \qquad \frac{14}{4} = \boxed{} \qquad \frac{2}{4} = \boxed{}$$

c)

$$\frac{2}{4} = \boxed{} \qquad \frac{12}{8} = \boxed{} \qquad \frac{14}{8} = \boxed{} \qquad \frac{3}{4} = \boxed{}$$

BONUS ▶ Use the number lines to find an equivalent fraction.

$$\frac{21}{2} = \boxed{}$$

COPYRIGHT © JUMP MATH: NOT TO BE COPIED. US EDITION

47. Whole Numbers as Fractions

You can write fractions for whole shapes.

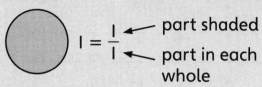

$1 = \dfrac{1}{1}$ ← part shaded ← part in each whole

$2 = \dfrac{2}{1}$ ← parts shaded ← part in each whole

1. Write the whole number as a fraction with the denominator 1.

a) $3 = \boxed{\dfrac{3}{1}}$ b) $6 = \boxed{}$ c) $8 = \boxed{}$ **BONUS** ▶ $99 = \boxed{}$

If you draw 2 parts in each whole, the whole number 2 can be written as the fraction $\dfrac{4}{2}$.

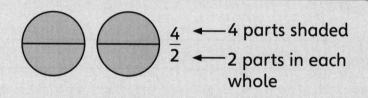

$\dfrac{4}{2}$ ← 4 parts shaded ← 2 parts in each whole

2. Write the whole number as a fraction with the denominator 2.

a) 3

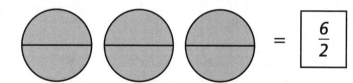

$= \boxed{\dfrac{6}{2}}$

b) 4

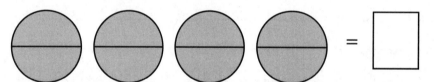

$= \boxed{}$

c) 5

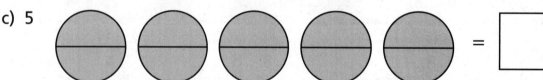

$= \boxed{}$

BONUS ▶ $10 = \boxed{}$

3. Write the whole number as a fraction with the denominator 3.

a) $2 = \dfrac{6}{3}$ b) $3 = \dfrac{}{3}$ c) $4 = \dfrac{}{3}$ **BONUS** ▶ $10 = \dfrac{}{3}$

COPYRIGHT © JUMP MATH: NOT TO BE COPIED. US EDITION

4. Write the whole numbers on the number line as fractions.

a)

$$\frac{0}{1} \qquad \frac{1}{1} \qquad \frac{2}{1} \qquad \boxed{\frac{3}{1}} \qquad \boxed{\frac{4}{1}} \qquad \boxed{\frac{5}{1}}$$

b)
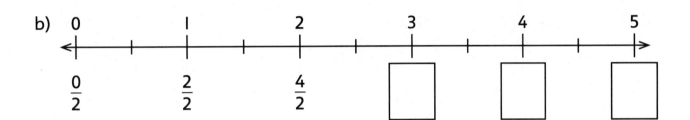

$$\frac{0}{2} \qquad \frac{2}{2} \qquad \frac{4}{2} \qquad \Box \qquad \Box \qquad \Box$$

c)
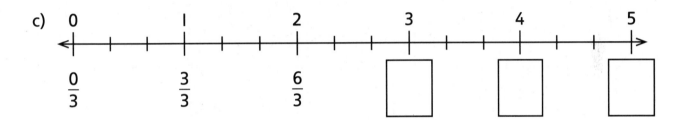

$$\frac{0}{3} \qquad \frac{3}{3} \qquad \frac{6}{3} \qquad \Box \qquad \Box \qquad \Box$$

d)
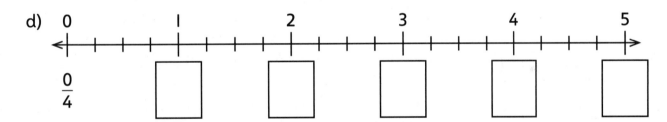

$$\frac{0}{4} \qquad \Box \qquad \Box \qquad \Box \qquad \Box \qquad \Box$$

e)
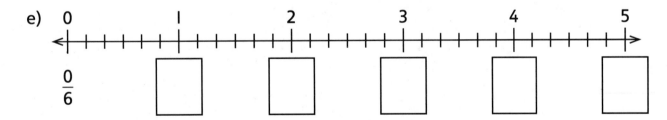

$$\frac{0}{6} \qquad \Box \qquad \Box \qquad \Box \qquad \Box \qquad \Box$$

BONUS ▶

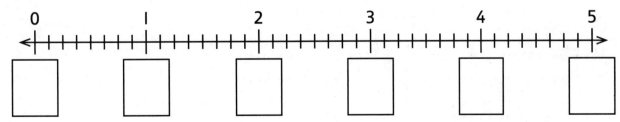

$$\Box \qquad \Box \qquad \Box \qquad \Box \qquad \Box \qquad \Box$$

COPYRIGHT © JUMP MATH: NOT TO BE COPIED. US EDITION

48. Mixed Numbers (Advanced)

Helen and her friends cut some pizzas into quarters.

They ate 11 of the quarters or $\frac{11}{4}$ pizzas.

In this fraction, the **numerator** is larger than the **denominator**.

The fraction represents more than one whole.
These kinds of fractions are called **improper fractions**.

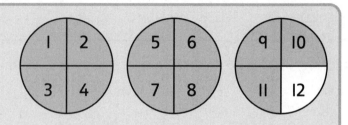

1. Write an improper fraction for the picture.

a) $\dfrac{9}{4}$

b)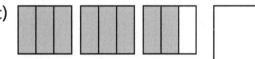

c)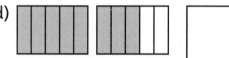

d)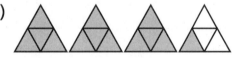

e)

f)

2. Write an improper fraction to label the dot.

a)  $\dfrac{7}{3}$

b)

c)

d)

BONUS ▶ Write an improper fraction for the picture.

COPYRIGHT © JUMP MATH: NOT TO BE COPIED. US EDITION

3. Shade one part at a time until the picture shows the given fraction.

a) $\frac{7}{4}$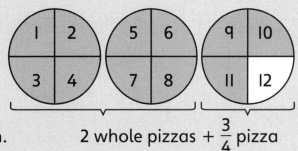

b) $\frac{10}{3}$

c) $\frac{5}{2}$

d) $\frac{19}{6}$

4. Place a dot on the number line to show the fraction.

a) $\frac{9}{4}$

b) $\frac{7}{2}$

c) $\frac{8}{3}$

d) $\frac{10}{6}$

Helen and her friends ate $\frac{11}{4}$ pizzas.

You can write $\frac{11}{4}$ as $2\frac{3}{4}$.

$2\frac{3}{4}$ is called a **mixed number** because it is a mixture of a whole number and a fraction.

2 whole pizzas $+ \frac{3}{4}$ pizza

5. Write the whole number and the fraction. Then write the mixed number.

a)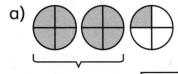

$\underline{\ \ 2\ \ }$ and $\boxed{\dfrac{1}{4}}$ = $\boxed{2\dfrac{1}{4}}$

b)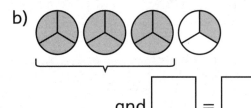

$\underline{\ \ \ \ \ }$ and $\boxed{}$ = $\boxed{}$

c)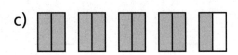

$\underline{\ \ \ \ \ }$ and $\boxed{}$ = $\boxed{}$

d)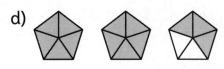

$\underline{\ \ \ \ \ }$ and $\boxed{}$ = $\boxed{}$

COPYRIGHT © JUMP MATH: NOT TO BE COPIED. US EDITION

6. Shade to show the mixed number.

a) $1\frac{3}{4}$

b) $3\frac{1}{3}$

c) $2\frac{5}{6}$

d) $3\frac{7}{9}$

7. Write a mixed number for the dot on the number line.

a)
```
0    1    2    3    4
```

[2] and [$\frac{1}{3}$] = [$2\frac{1}{3}$]

b)
```
0        1        2        3
```

[ ] and [ ] = [ ]

c)
```
0  1  2  3  4  5  6
```

[ ] and [ ] = [ ]

d)
```
0            1            2
```

[ ] and [ ] = [ ]

8. Write an improper fraction and a mixed number for the picture.

Improper Fraction   **Mixed Number**

a)

[ ]   [ ]

b)

[ ]   [ ]

c)

[ ]   [ ]

BONUS ▶ What improper fraction is equal to $10\frac{1}{2}$? _____

COPYRIGHT © JUMP MATH: NOT TO BE COPIED. US EDITION

49. Fractions with the Same Denominator

REMINDER ▸ $\frac{2}{3}$ ← The numerator tells you how many parts are shaded
← The denominator tells you how many equal parts are in the whole.

1. Write the fraction that is shaded in each shape. Circle the larger fraction.

a) 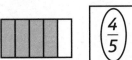 $\frac{2}{5}$
   $\boxed{\frac{4}{5}}$

b)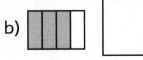
   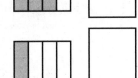

c)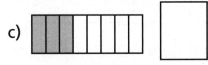
   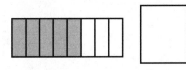

d)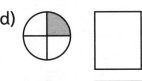
   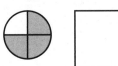

e)

f)
   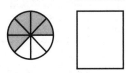

2. Write a fraction for the dot on each number line. Circle the larger fraction.

a)

b)
   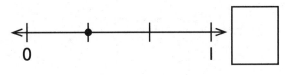

c)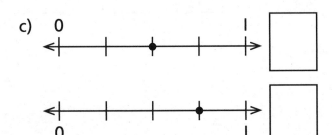

d)

3. Circle the correct word.

In each pair of fractions on this page, the   numerators / denominators
are the same.

COPYRIGHT © JUMP MATH: NOT TO BE COPIED. US EDITION

$\dfrac{4}{5}$ ←——— The denominators ———→ $\dfrac{2}{5}$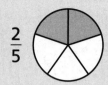
are the same.

The numerator of $\dfrac{4}{5}$ is greater than the numerator of $\dfrac{2}{5}$.

More parts are shaded in $\dfrac{4}{5}$ than in $\dfrac{2}{5}$, so $\dfrac{4}{5} > \dfrac{2}{5}$.

4. Compare the numerators. Then circle the larger fraction.

a) $\dfrac{3}{5}$ or $\dfrac{1}{5}$ b) $\dfrac{4}{7}$ or $\dfrac{6}{7}$ c) $\dfrac{7}{8}$ or $\dfrac{1}{8}$ **BONUS** ▶ $\dfrac{38}{75}$ or $\dfrac{21}{75}$

5. Compare the numerators and write the fractions in order from largest to smallest.

a) $\dfrac{3}{4}$ $\dfrac{1}{4}$ $\dfrac{2}{4}$
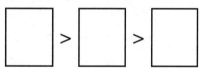

b) $\dfrac{5}{8}$ $\dfrac{7}{8}$ $\dfrac{1}{8}$ $\dfrac{8}{8}$
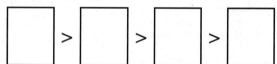

6. Compare the numerators and write the fractions in order from smallest to largest.

a) $\dfrac{4}{5}$ $\dfrac{2}{5}$ $\dfrac{5}{5}$
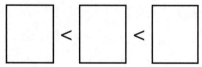

b) $\dfrac{7}{16}$ $\dfrac{1}{16}$ $\dfrac{11}{16}$ $\dfrac{14}{16}$
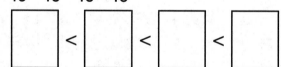

7. Write the missing fractions with the denominator 11.

$\dfrac{9}{11} >$ ☐ $> \dfrac{7}{11} >$ ☐ $> \dfrac{5}{11}$

8. Write a fraction between the two fractions.

a) $\dfrac{3}{7}$ and $\dfrac{5}{7}$ b) $\dfrac{9}{12}$ and $\dfrac{7}{12}$ c) $\dfrac{10}{16}$ and $\dfrac{12}{16}$ **BONUS** ▶ $\dfrac{95}{100}$ and $\dfrac{97}{100}$

COPYRIGHT © JUMP MATH: NOT TO BE COPIED. US EDITION

50. Fractions with the Same Numerator

I. Write the fraction that is shaded. Circle the larger fraction.

a)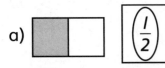

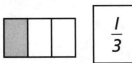

b)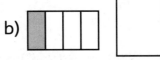

c)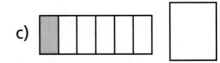

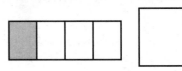

d)

e)

f)

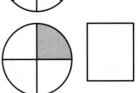

2. Write a fraction for the dot on each number line. Circle the larger fraction.

a)

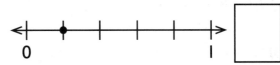

b)

c)

d)

3. Circle the correct word.

In each pair of fractions on this page, the   numerators / denominators
are the same.

COPYRIGHT © JUMP MATH: NOT TO BE COPIED. US EDITION

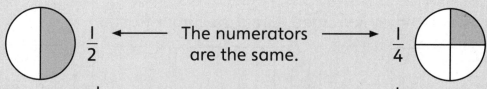

The denominator of $\frac{1}{2}$ is smaller than the denominator of $\frac{1}{4}$.

Each equal part in $\frac{1}{2}$ is larger than each equal part in $\frac{1}{4}$, so $\frac{1}{2} > \frac{1}{4}$.

4. Compare the denominators. Then circle the larger fraction.

a) $\frac{1}{4}$ or $\frac{1}{3}$

b) $\frac{1}{4}$ or $\frac{1}{8}$

c) $\frac{1}{6}$ or $\frac{1}{8}$

d) $\frac{1}{2}$ or $\frac{1}{5}$

e) $\frac{1}{3}$ or $\frac{1}{16}$

BONUS ▶ $\frac{1}{8}$ or $\frac{1}{99}$

$\frac{2}{3} > \frac{2}{4}$ because each part in $\frac{2}{3}$ is larger than each part in $\frac{2}{4}$.

5. Compare the denominators. Then circle the larger fraction.

a) $\frac{2}{4}$ or $\frac{2}{5}$

b) $\frac{3}{8}$ or $\frac{3}{4}$

c) $\frac{5}{8}$ or $\frac{5}{6}$

d) $\frac{2}{6}$ or $\frac{2}{3}$

e) $\frac{3}{4}$ or $\frac{3}{16}$

BONUS ▶ $\frac{7}{8}$ or $\frac{7}{88}$

6. Compare the denominators. Then write the fractions in order from largest to smallest.

a) $\frac{1}{4}$ $\frac{1}{2}$ $\frac{1}{3}$ ☐ > ☐ > ☐

b) $\frac{1}{8}$ $\frac{1}{6}$ $\frac{1}{2}$ ☐ > ☐ > ☐

c) $\frac{3}{4}$ $\frac{3}{6}$ $\frac{3}{8}$ ☐ > ☐ > ☐

d) $\frac{5}{6}$ $\frac{5}{10}$ $\frac{5}{8}$ ☐ > ☐ > ☐

COPYRIGHT © JUMP MATH: NOT TO BE COPIED. US EDITION

51. Puzzles and Problems

1. John ate $\frac{3}{4}$ of a pie. What fraction of a pie is left? Explain using a picture.

2. Is one half of Picture A the same as one half of Picture B? _____

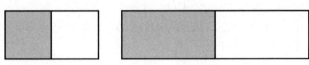

    Picture A   Picture B

Explain. _____

_____

3. Shade $\frac{3}{4}$ of the picture.

a) 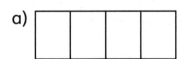   b)    c)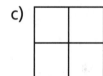

4. Use the pictures to explain why $\frac{1}{2} = \frac{2}{4}$.

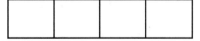

5. Use the number lines to explain why $\frac{1}{3} = \frac{2}{6}$.

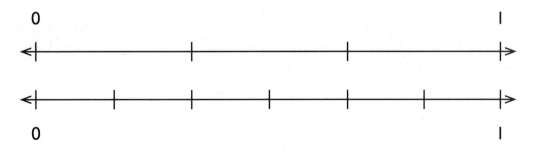

COPYRIGHT © JUMP MATH: NOT TO BE COPIED. US EDITION

6. a) Write an improper fraction for the picture.

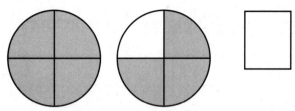

b) Write a mixed number for the picture.

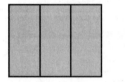 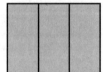 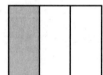

7. Circle the larger fraction.

a) $\dfrac{3}{8}$ or $\dfrac{5}{8}$ b) $\dfrac{1}{2}$ or $\dfrac{1}{3}$ c) $\dfrac{2}{5}$ or $\dfrac{2}{3}$

8. Ava, Sun, Ravi, and Will share a pizza. Ava and Sun each take $\dfrac{1}{3}$ of the pizza. Ravi and Will split the last piece.

a) What fraction of the pizza did Ava and Sun eat altogether?

b) What fraction of the pizza is left for Ravi and Will?

c) What fraction did Ravi and Will each get?

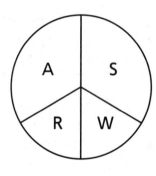

9. What fraction of the whole square is each labeled part?

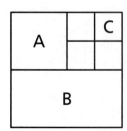   A = ☐   B = ☐   **BONUS ▶** C = ☐

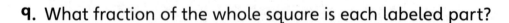

COPYRIGHT © JUMP MATH: NOT TO BE COPIED. US EDITION

52. Equal and Not Equal

1. Write the number of balls on each table. Write = if the tables have the same number. Write ≠ if they do not have the same number.

a)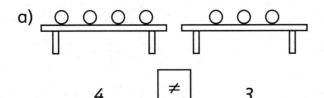

4   ≠   3

b)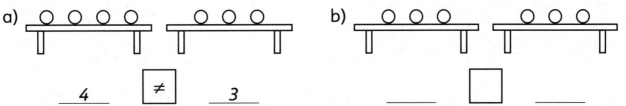

___   ☐   ___

c)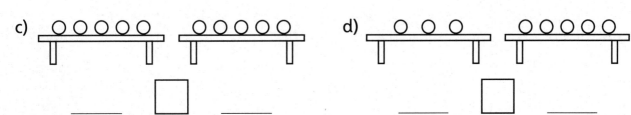

___   ☐   ___

d)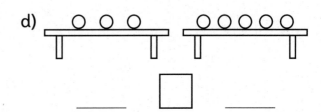

___   ☐   ___

2. Write the number of balls. Write = or ≠ in the box.

a)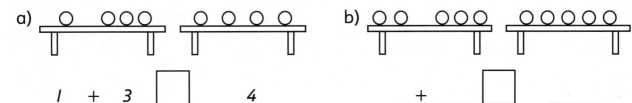

1 + 3   ☐   4

b)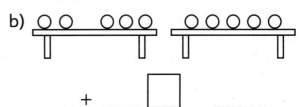

___ + ___   ☐   ___

c)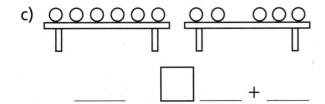

___   ☐   ___ + ___

d)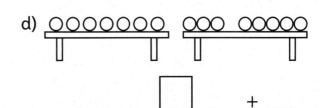

___   ☐   ___ + ___

e)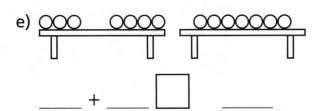

___ + ___   ☐   ___

f)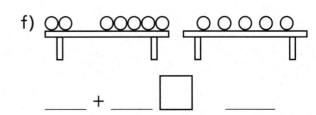

___ + ___   ☐   ___

g)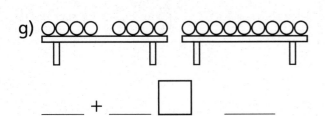

___ + ___   ☐   ___

h)

___   ☐   ___ + ___

COPYRIGHT © JUMP MATH: NOT TO BE COPIED. US EDITION

3. Circle the correct addition sentence.

a) (7 = 3 + 4)

    7 ≠ 3 + 4

b) 9 = 5 + 3

    (9 ≠ 5 + 3)

c) 8 = 6 + 2

    8 ≠ 6 + 2

d) 5 = 3 + 1

    5 ≠ 3 + 1

e) 11 + 5 = 16

    11 + 5 ≠ 16

f) 12 + 3 = 15

    12 + 3 ≠ 15

An **equation** is a number sentence that has an **equal sign** (=).

$$3 + 5 = 8$$

    ↑

equal sign

The equal sign shows that the left side of the number sentence has the same value as the right side.

---

4. Circle the number sentences that are equations.

A. 5 + 7 ≠ 13   **B.** 6 < 9   **C.** 15 − 2 = 13

D. 4 = 32 ÷ 8   **E.** 6 × 5 > 15   **F.** 14 ≠ 12 + 3

5. Write "T" if the equation is true. Write "F" if the equation is false.

a) 3 + 7 = 10   _T_   b) 9 + 4 = 12   _F_   c) 2 + 17 = 18 _____

d) 6 − 2 = 4 _____   e) 24 − 5 = 19 _____   f) 25 − 13 = 11 _____

g) 3 × 9 = 27 _____   h) 6 × 7 = 42 _____   i) 56 = 8 × 8 _____

j) 24 ÷ 4 = 8 _____   k) 12 ÷ 3 = 4 _____   l) 6 = 35 ÷ 5 _____

m) 14 + 13 = 27 _____   n) 9 × 3 = 28 _____   o) 9 = 45 ÷ 5 _____

p) 18 − 12 = 7 _____   q) 4 = 15 − 10 _____   r) 8 = 80 ÷ 10 _____

BONUS ▶

s) 2 + 4 = 3 × 2 _____   t) 5 + 6 = 14 − 2 _____   u) 24 ÷ 6 = 10 − 6 _____

COPYRIGHT © JUMP MATH: NOT TO BE COPIED. US EDITION

53. Unknown Numbers in Equations (1)

1. Some apples are inside a box and some are outside. Draw the missing apples in the box.

a) (total number of apples)

b)

c)

d)

2. Draw the missing apples in the box. Then write the missing number in the smaller box.

a)

$$5 = 3 + \boxed{2}$$

b)

$$8 = 3 + \boxed{}$$

c)

$$3 + \boxed{} = 4$$

d)

$$4 + \boxed{} = 7$$

> Finding the missing number in an equation is called **solving** the equation.

3. Draw a picture for the equation. Use your picture to solve the equation.

a) $5 + \boxed{} = 6$

b) $\boxed{} + 4 = 9$

COPYRIGHT © JUMP MATH: NOT TO BE COPIED. US EDITION

54. Using Letters for Unknown Numbers

I. Solve the equation by guessing and checking.

a) $\boxed{} + 3 = 4$

b) $\boxed{} + 3 = 5$

c) $\boxed{} + 5 = 7$

d) $2 + \boxed{} = 6$

e) $2 + \boxed{} = 7$

f) $8 = \boxed{} + 5$

2. Sam took some apples from a box. Write how many apples were in the box before.

a)

$\boxed{7}$ – =

Sam took away this many.　　This many were left.

b)

$\boxed{}$ – =

c)

$\boxed{}$ – =

d)

= $\boxed{}$ –

3. Solve the equation by guessing and checking.

a) $\boxed{} - 2 = 2$

b) $\boxed{} - 4 = 3$

c) $\boxed{} - 3 = 3$

d) $5 - \boxed{} = 1$

e) $7 - \boxed{} = 2$

f) $6 - \boxed{} = 4$

> You can use a letter to stand for the number you do not know.
>
> $\boxed{} + 5 = 8$ can be written as $x + 5 = 8$ or $b + 5 = 8$.

4. Solve the equation.

a) $x + 3 = 5$

b) $x + 7 = 10$

c) $x - 2 = 5$

$x = \underline{}$

$x = \underline{}$

$x = \underline{}$

d) $10 - a = 6$

e) $4 + y = 9$

f) $11 = m + 3$

$a = \underline{}$

$y = \underline{}$

$m = \underline{}$

COPYRIGHT © JUMP MATH: NOT TO BE COPIED. US EDITION

55. Unknown Numbers in Equations (2)

I. Draw the same number of apples in each box. Write the equation for the picture.

a)

$$\square + \square = 8$$

b)

$$\square + \square + \square = 9$$

c)

$$\square + \square + \square = 15$$

> **REMINDER ▶**
>
> Multiplication is a short form for repeated addition.
>
> 2 + 2 + 2 is the same as 3×2
>
> is the same as $3 \times$

2. Draw the missing apples in the box. Then write the missing number in the smaller box.

a)

$$3 \times \boxed{2} = 6$$

b)

$$2 \times \boxed{} = 8$$

c)

$$3 \times \boxed{} = 15$$

d)

$$6 \times \boxed{} = 18$$

COPYRIGHT © JUMP MATH: NOT TO BE COPIED. US EDITION

3. How many apples should be in the box? Write the number.

a) $2 \times \boxed{3} = $ 🍎🍎🍎 🍎🍎🍎

b) $2 \times \boxed{} = $ 🍎🍎 🍎🍎

c) $\boxed{} \times 3 = $ 🍎🍎🍎 🍎🍎🍎

d) $\boxed{} \times 4 = $ 🍎🍎🍎🍎 🍎🍎🍎🍎

e) $\boxed{} \times 5 = $ 🍎🍎🍎🍎🍎 🍎🍎🍎🍎🍎

f) $\boxed{} \times 2 = $ 🍎🍎🍎🍎 🍎🍎🍎🍎

g) $3 \times$ 🍎🍎🍎 🍎🍎🍎 $= \boxed{}$

h) $8 \times$ 🍎🍎 🍎🍎 $= \boxed{}$

4. Solve the equation.

a) $5 \times \boxed{} = 10$

b) $4 \times \boxed{} = 12$

c) $\boxed{} \times 3 = 21$

d) $8 \times \boxed{} = 64$

e) $\boxed{} \times 9 = 27$

f) $14 = \boxed{} \times 2$

g) $\boxed{} \div 3 = 2$

h) $\boxed{} \div 4 = 4$

i) $\boxed{} \div 5 = 7$

j) $\boxed{} \div 6 = 7$

k) $\boxed{} \div 8 = 6$

l) $28 = \boxed{} \times 7$

5. Solve the equation.

a) $3 \times a = 18$

b) $4 \times b = 20$

c) $b \times 3 = 21$

$a = $ _____

$b = $ _____

$b = $ _____

d) $y \times 6 = 42$

e) $5 \times t = 25$

BONUS ▶ $a + a = 12$

$y = $ _____

$t = $ _____

$a = $ _____

COPYRIGHT © JUMP MATH: NOT TO BE COPIED. US EDITION

56. Equations with Unknowns and Word Problems

You can write a story for an addition equation.

Example: ☐ + 2 = 5

Story: Peter had some stickers.
His friend gave him 2 more stickers.
Now Peter has 5 stickers in total.

1. Write a story for the equation.

a) ☐ + 2 = 7

_____

_____

b) ☐ + 4 = 8

_____

_____

_____

You can write a story for a multiplication equation.

Example: 3 × ☐ = 12

Story: There are 3 boxes.
Each box has the same number of apples.
There are 12 apples altogether.

2. Write a story for the equation.

a) 4 × ☐ = 8

b) 2 × ☐ = 6

c) 5 × ☐ = 35

BONUS ▶ ☐ − 2 = 6

BONUS ▶ Write an equation for the story. Solve the equation.

a) Kim had some apples.
She bought 3 more apples.
Now she has 8 apples altogether.

b) There are 4 boxes.
Each box has the same
number of oranges.
There are 8 oranges altogether.

COPYRIGHT © JUMP MATH: NOT TO BE COPIED. US EDITION

57. Tape Diagrams (1)

Jane draws a **tape diagram** to compare the numbers 10 and 6.

She draws 2 **bars** and labels them.　　She adds 10 + 6 to find the total.

She subtracts 10 − 6 to find the difference.

10
6

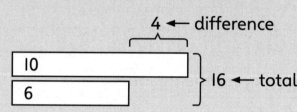

1. Fill in the total or the missing number.

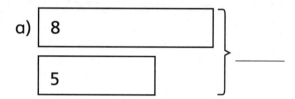

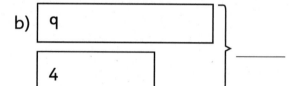

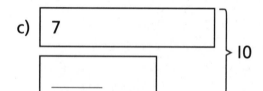

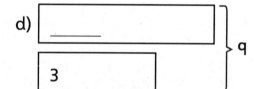

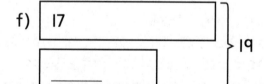

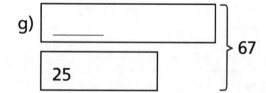

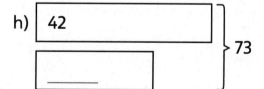

BONUS ▶

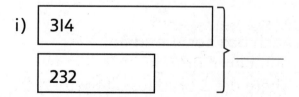

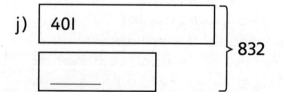

COPYRIGHT © JUMP MATH: NOT TO BE COPIED. US EDITION

2. Fill in the difference or the missing number.

a)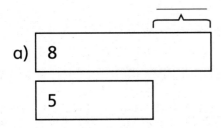

b)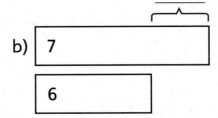

c)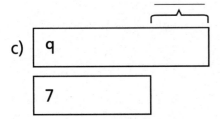

d)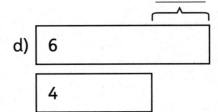

e)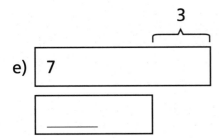

f)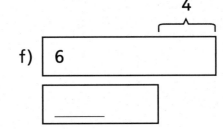

3. Find the missing number.

a)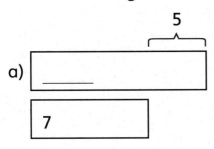

b)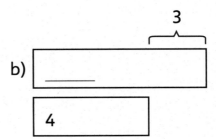

c)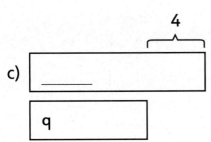

d)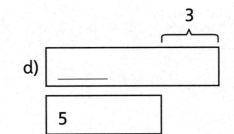

COPYRIGHT © JUMP MATH: NOT TO BE COPIED. US EDITION

4. Fill in the blanks.

a)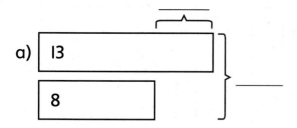

b)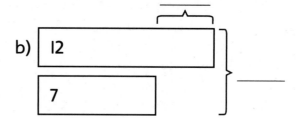

c)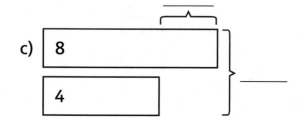

d)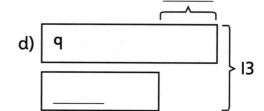

e)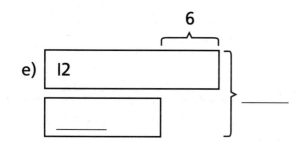

f)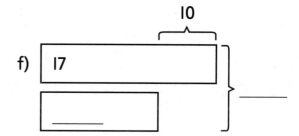

g)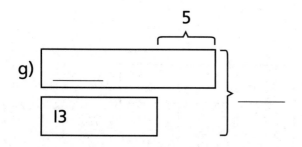

h)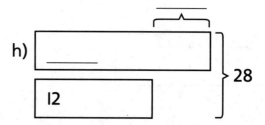

COPYRIGHT © JUMP MATH: NOT TO BE COPIED. US EDITION

BONUS ▶

i)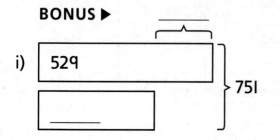

j)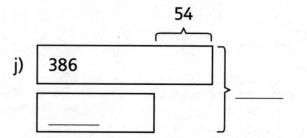

JUMP Math Accumula

58. Tape Diagrams (2)

I. Underline the part that is larger. Write the name of that part beside the longer bar. Fill in the blanks.

a) 8 <u>apples</u> and 5 oranges

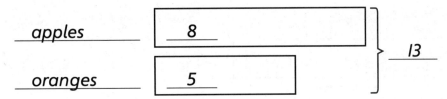

apples   8

oranges   5   13

b) 4 red fish and 9 blue fish

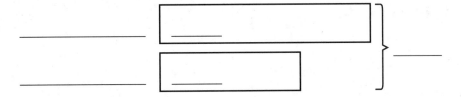

c) 13 pens and 12 pencils

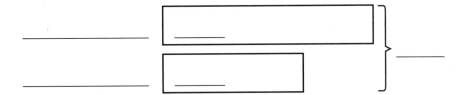

d) 11 plates and 16 cups

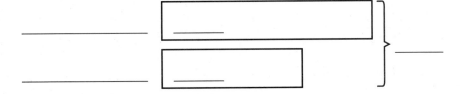

BONUS ▶ 9 apples in total
5 are red and the rest are green

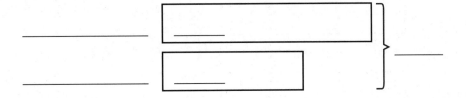

COPYRIGHT © JUMP MATH: NOT TO BE COPIED. US EDITION

2. Underline the part that is larger. Write the name of that part beside the longer bar. Fill in the blanks.

a) 3 more cats than dogs
   5 dogs

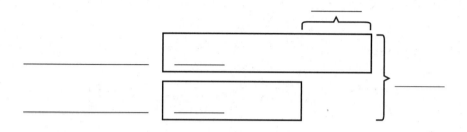

b) 10 more spoons than forks
   4 forks

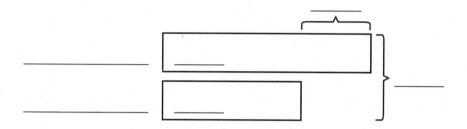

c) 4 fewer girls than boys
   12 boys

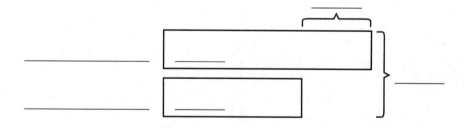

d) 6 fewer science books than art books
   8 science books

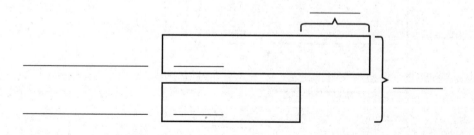

COPYRIGHT © JUMP MATH: NOT TO BE COPIED. US EDITION

3. Fill in the blanks.

a) 9 lions and 7 tigers

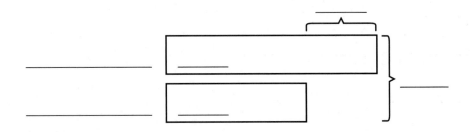

b) 9 more girls than boys
13 girls

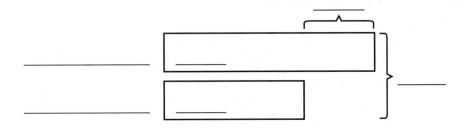

c) 6 more boys than girls
5 girls

BONUS ▶ Karen has 12 apples in total.
8 are green. The others are red.

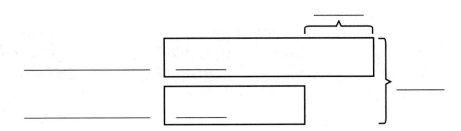

COPYRIGHT © JUMP MATH: NOT TO BE COPIED. US EDITION

4. There are 24 students in a class. 14 are boys.

a) Fill in the blanks.

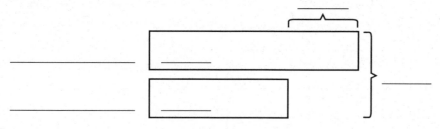

b) How many girls are in the class? _____

c) How many more boys than girls are there? _____

5. Alan has 5 more US stamps than Canadian stamps.
He has 12 Canadian stamps.

a) Fill in the blanks.

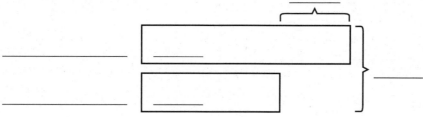

b) How many stamps does he have in total? _____

6. Sally rode her bike 252 miles to raise money for charity.
Kevin rode his bike 57 miles.

a) Draw a tape diagram to show this information.

b) How much farther did Sally ride?

c) How many miles did they ride altogether?

BONUS ▶ Hint: Use a tape diagram with 3 bars.

a) A store sold 8 books on Friday.
They sold 5 fewer books on Thursday than on Friday.
They sold 4 more books on Saturday than on Friday.
How many books did the store sell on the three days?

b) Ivan has 12 green apples.
He has 7 more red apples than green apples.
He has 3 fewer yellow apples than red apples.
How many apples does he have altogether?

Books
for sale

COPYRIGHT © JUMP MATH: NOT TO BE COPIED. US EDITION

59. Rows and Columns

REMINDER ▶ An array has rows and columns of objects, like squares or dots.

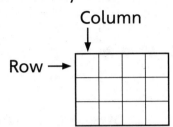

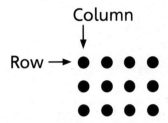

1. Number the rows and columns. Write the total number of small squares in the array.

a)

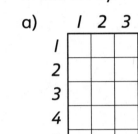

    __5__ rows

    __3__ columns

    total __5 × 3 = 15__

    or __3 × 5 = 15__

b)

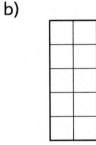

    _____ rows

    _____ columns

    total _____

    or _____

c)

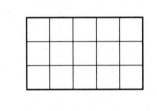

    _____ rows

    _____ columns

    total _____

    or _____

2. Count the rows and columns. Write the total number of dots in the array.

a)

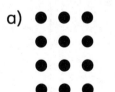

    __4__ rows

    __3__ columns

    total __4 × 3 = 12__

    or __3 × 4 = 12__

b)

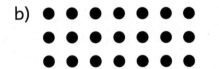

    _____ rows

    _____ columns

    total _____

    or _____

c)

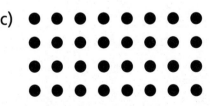

    _____ rows

    _____ columns

    total _____

    or _____

COPYRIGHT © JUMP MATH: NOT TO BE COPIED. US EDITION

3. Write a multiplication equation for the total number of dots.
Then write another multiplication equation and two division
equations for the array.

a)
● ● ● ● ●
● ● ● ● ●
● ● ● ● ●

____3____ rows ____5____ columns

total ___3 × 5 = 15___

___5 × 3 = 15___

___15 ÷ 5 = 3___

___15 ÷ 3 = 5___

b)
● ● ● ● ● ●
● ● ● ● ● ●

_____ rows _____ columns

total _____

_____

_____

_____

4. The table gives the number of rows and columns for arrays.
Write two multiplication equations and two division equations
for each array.

	Rows	Columns	Total	Equations		
a)	5	2	10	5 × 2 = 10 2 × 5 = 10	10 ÷ 5 = 2 10 ÷ 2 = 5	
b)	6	4	24			
c)	3	7	21			
d)	7	8	56			
e)	8	6	48			
f)	10	9	90			

COPYRIGHT © JUMP MATH: NOT TO BE COPIED. US EDITION

5. The question mark (?) is the number we do not know. Write an equation that gives the unknown.

	Rows	Columns	Total	Equation
a)	3	5	?	$? = 3 \times 5$
b)	?	6	18	$? = 18 \div 6$
c)	?	2	16	
d)	4	?	36	
e)	7	8	?	
f)	9	?	45	

6. Ken plants 8 rows of trees. He plants 3 trees in each row. How many trees does he plant? Draw an array of dots to show your answer.

7. Randi arranges 35 chairs in rows with 5 chairs in each row. How many rows of chairs did she make?

8. Beth plants 12 flowers in 3 rows. How many flowers are in each row?

9. Mona arranges 9 rows of beads with 7 beads in each row. How many beads are in her array?

BONUS ▶ John makes an array using dimes.
He makes 2 rows with 4 dimes in each row.

a) How many dimes did John use?

b) How much money did John use?

BONUS ▶ Marco plants 6 rows of trees with 4 in each row.
Tom plants 7 rows of trees with 3 in each row.
How many more trees did Marco plant?

BONUS ▶ Wendy arranges 36 stickers with 6 in each row.
Raj arranges 49 stickers with 7 in each row.
Who made more rows?

COPYRIGHT © JUMP MATH: NOT TO BE COPIED. US EDITION

60. Problems with Multiplication and Division

1. Write two multiplication equations and two division equations for the picture.

a)

___2___ groups

___3___ in each group

___6___ in total

___2 × 3 = 6___

___3 × 2 = 6___

___6 ÷ 2 = 3___

___6 ÷ 3 = 2___

b)

_____ groups

_____ in each group

_____ in total

_____

_____

_____

_____

c)

_____ groups

_____ in each group

_____ in total

_____

_____

_____

_____

2. Write two multiplication equations and two division equations for each row in the table.

	Number of Groups	Number in Each Group	Total	Equations	
a)	3	7	21	3 × 7 = 21 7 × 3 = 21	21 ÷ 3 = 7 21 ÷ 7 = 3
b)	9	5	45		
c)	7	6	42		
d)	8	4	32		

COPYRIGHT © JUMP MATH: NOT TO BE COPIED. US EDITION

3. Write a question mark (?) for the amount you do not know.
Then write an equation that solves the problem.

	Problem	Number of Groups	Number in Each Group	Total	Equation
a)	3 pears in each basket 12 pears How many baskets?	?	3	12	? = 12 ÷ 3
b)	4 toys in each box 6 boxes How many toys?				
c)	5 birds on each branch 35 birds How many branches?				
d)	3 children in each boat 12 children in total How many boats?				
e)	3 tents 15 children How many children in each tent?				
f)	5 rows of trees 40 trees How many in each row?				
g)	30 bananas 6 bananas in each bag How many bags?				
h)	9 pennies in each pocket 4 pockets How many pennies in total?				

COPYRIGHT © JUMP MATH: NOT TO BE COPIED. US EDITION

4. There are 2 hamsters in each classroom. How many hamsters are in 8 classrooms?

5. Clara bought 24 stamps. There are 8 stamps in each pack. How many packs did she buy?

6. Anwar put 32 granola bars in 8 boxes. He put the same number in each box. How many did he put in each box?

7. Zack bought 8 packs of pens with 5 pens in each pack. Yu bought 9 packs of pens with 4 pens in each pack.

   a) How many pens did Zack buy?

   b) How many pens did Yu buy?

   c) Who bought more pens?

8. Alex planted 24 flowers with 3 in each row. Marco planted 42 flowers with 6 in each row. Who planted more rows?

9. Rani planted 18 trees in 3 rows. Nina planted 24 trees in 6 rows. How many more trees are in Rani's rows than in Nina's rows?

10. A chess team has 4 players. School A sent 20 players to a chess match. School B sent 32 players to the match. How many more teams did School B send?

11. A basketball team has 5 players. School A sent 7 teams to a basketball match. School B sent 8 teams to the match. How many players did School A and School B send altogether?

BONUS ▶ A rubber raft costs $8 and can hold 3 children. There are 12 children who want to buy rafts.

   a) How many rafts should the children buy?

   b) How much will all the rafts cost?

COPYRIGHT © JUMP MATH: NOT TO BE COPIED. US EDITION

61. Multistep Problems

1. Mark has 28 pears. He eats 4 and gives the rest to 3 friends. Each friend gets the same number of pears.

a) How many pears are left after Mark eats 4 of them?

b) How many pears does each of Mark's friends get?

2. Anna has 12 books. Then she buys 6 more and puts all the books in 3 boxes. She puts the same number of books in each box.

a) How many books does Anna have in total?

b) How many books does she put in each box?

3. 32 children go camping. They put up 6 tents. Each tent holds 4 children.

a) How many tents do 32 children need?

b) How many more tents do they need to put up?

4. Mary has 23 fossils and Ben has 25 fossils. They put all their fossils in a display case. If they put 8 fossils on each shelf, how many shelves do they use?

5. 6 students want to buy pizzas for a school party. Each student has $5. A pizza costs $10. How many pizzas can they buy?

6. Lucy earns $10 each week shoveling snow. She spends $4 each week and saves the rest of her money. How much money will she save in 3 weeks?

7. Amy earns $15 each week doing chores. She spends $7 each week and saves the rest of her money. How much money will she save in 9 weeks?

BONUS ▶ 4 children pick 20 apples and share them equally. Each child eats 2 apples.

a) How many apples does each child have after they eat the apples?

b) How many apples do they now have in total?

COPYRIGHT © JUMP MATH: NOT TO BE COPIED. US EDITION

8. Anna has 9 five-dollar bills. Ravi has 7 ten-dollar bills.

   a) How much money does Anna have?

   b) How much money does Ravi have?

   c) How much money do they have altogether?

9. Kate has 4 five-dollar bills. She wants to buy 7 light bulbs. Each light bulb costs $3.

   a) How much money does Kate have?

   b) How much do 7 light bulbs cost?

   c) Does she have enough money to buy the bulbs?

10. Tim bought 30 stamps in packs of 6. Josh bought 32 stamps in packs of 8. Who bought more packs of stamps?

11. Ben ran 10 blocks on Saturday and 7 blocks on Sunday. Zara ran 8 blocks on Saturday and 11 blocks on Sunday. Who ran more, Ben or Zara?

12. Jon plants 3 rows of flowers with 7 in each row. Alexa plants 8 rows of flowers with 5 in each row. How many flowers do they plant altogether?

13. Ellen buys 9 crayons that cost 8¢ each. Ava buys 7 erasers that cost 10¢ each. How much more money does Ellen spend than Ava?

14. Zack buys 10 pencils that cost 6 cents each. Ali buys 4 pens that cost 9 cents each. How much money do Zack and Ali spend altogether?

BONUS ▶ Ed slices 18 mushrooms to add to 3 pizzas. Ross uses 24 mushrooms for 6 pizzas.

   a) Who uses more mushrooms for 1 pizza?

   b) If Ross and Ed each make 1 pizza, how many mushrooms will they need?

COPYRIGHT © JUMP MATH: NOT TO BE COPIED. US EDITION

62. More Multistep Problems (Advanced)

When you solve a word problem, you can use brackets to show what happens first.

A teacher has 21 stickers. She buys 4 more. Then 5 of her students share them equally.

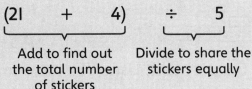

(21 + 4) ÷ 5

Add to find out the total number of stickers

Divide to share the stickers equally

1. Use brackets to show what happens first.

a) A teacher has 25 stickers.
She buys 5 more.
Then she shares them equally among 6 students.

___(25 + 5) ÷ 6___

b) A teacher has 19 books.
He buys 8 more.
Then he shares them equally among 9 students.

_____

c) There are 9 pumpkins in a garden.
3 more grow.
4 children share them equally.

_____

d) Kyle has 14 plums.
He eats 2.
Then he gives the rest to 3 friends to share equally.

_____

e) Sarah has 19 bananas.
She eats 1.
6 monkeys share the rest equally.

_____

f) Ali has 3 muffins.
He bakes 12 more.
5 friends share the muffins equally.

_____

BONUS ▶

g) 9 children have 20 pencils.
They use 2 of them.
They share the pencils that are left equally.

_____

h) 8 children have 12 apples.
They pick 4 more.
Then they share them equally.

_____

COPYRIGHT © JUMP MATH: NOT TO BE COPIED. US EDITION

Use brackets to show which operation is done first.

Paul has 7 boxes.
There are 3 pens in each box.
He puts 2 more pens in each box.
How many pens are in the boxes now?

Number of pens = (3 + 2) × 7

2. Write an equation for the problem. Use x for the number you are trying to find.

a) A farmer has 3 barns.
There are 6 cows in each barn.
The farmer lets 2 more cows into each barn.
How many cows are in the barns now?

x = __(6 + 2) × 3__

b) Helen has 4 brothers.
Each brother has 3 stickers.
She gives each brother 5 more stickers.
How many stickers do the brothers have now?

x = _____

c) Sara buys 6 books for $4 each.
She buys a book bag for $10.
How much did she spend?

x = _____

d) Bev buys 5 tennis balls for $3 each.
Then she buys a tennis racket for $50.
How much did she spend?

x = _____

3. Write an equation and find the answer.

a) Jen keeps 5 fish in each of 5 aquariums.
She adds 2 more fish to each aquarium.
How many fish does she have now?

x = __(5 + 2) × 5__

x = __7 × 5__

x = __35__

b) There are 6 gardens.
Each garden has 3 flowers.
5 more flowers grow in each garden.
How many flowers are there now?

x = _____

x = _____

x = _____

COPYRIGHT © JUMP MATH: NOT TO BE COPIED. US EDITION